HINDU-MUSLIM UNITY AND LOVE FOR INDIA

HINDU-MUSLIM UNITY AND LOVE FOR INDIA

Khwaja Abdul Muntaqim

KALPAZ

ISBN : 978-93-5128-040-8

Price : ₹ 840

First Published, 2014

Published by

Kalpaz Publications
C-30, Satyawati Nagar,
Delhi-110052
Ph.: 9212142040
E-mail: kalpaz@hotmail.com

Laser Typesetting : Gyan Print (AB-II), Delhi
Printed at : G. Print Process, Delhi

Cataloging in Publication Data—DK
Courtesy: D.K. Agencies (P) Ltd. <docinfo@dkagencies.com>

Muntaqim, Khwaja A. (Khwaja Abdul)
Hindu Muslim unity and love for India / Khwajaabdul Muntaqim.
p. cm.
ISBN 9789351280408

1. Communalism—India. 2. Hindus—India. 3. Muslims—India. 4. Nationalism—India. 5. Nationalism—Religious aspects. I. Title.

DDC 302.14 23

Contents

Preface

The title of the book is self-explanatory. During my nine months stay in the United States of America, a multi-civilisational, multi-cultural, multi-creedal,multi-religious, multi-denominational,multi-lingual,multi-segmental and multi-diversified state like India, I was so impressed with its pluralistic character and cohesiveness that I decided to write a book on Hindu Muslim Unity and pluralistic society in my own country that is, India. I also refreshed my memory and re-collected the words of Gandhi Ji, contained in the article on Hindu-Muslim Unity written by him in the first quarter of 20th century. To quote:

"That unity is strength is not merely a copybook maxim but a rule of life is in no case so clearly illustrated as in the problem of Hindu-Muslim unity. Divided we must fall....... Hindu-Muslim unity means not unity only between Hindus and Muslims, but between all those who believe India to be their home, no matter to what faith they belong..........."

Hindu-Muslim Unity is the need of the hour and it is as much needed today as it was about hundred years ago. There is no religion in the world or there are no rules of ethics that do not speak of love, compassion, justice, freedom, peace, co-existence, honesty, liberty, dignity, fairness, mercy, tolerance, mutual respect, communal harmony, truth, non-violence and service to the society.All these values flow from and are core essence of all religions and ethical norms and it is the people, may not be all, who have been practicing contrary to what is contained in their religious scriptures or rules of ethics. They should sit together and draw up an agenda to make the message feasibly communicable so that it reaches the people and it ultimately becomes the voice of the people because *vox populi vox dei*, an Italian proverbial aphorism of common political wisdom, ultimately rules the scene.

There may be hundred reasons to hate each other but the balance shall always tilt in favour of innumerable reasons to love each other. The very purpose of life is to be happy and desire for peace and contentment. The more we care for the happiness and well-being of others and the more warm-hearted feelings we have for others the greater is our own sense of happiness,well-being and contentment and it helps us in reposing faith and confidence in each other and removing mutual misunderstandings generally based on unfounded grounds. The people must understand that religion is also a moral code and moral codes may differ. They should learn to live with a difference. It is not important whether the teachings of all religions are the same or not. These moral codes and beliefs should not divide the people.

Let the masses realize that Hindus and Muslims have to live and co-exist in India even if some of them hate some of them or all of them hate some of them or some of them hate all of them or some of them love them as individuals and not as a community or some of them remain indifferent. Some of us have to take the initiative. It is the constitutional duty of the majority and minority communities to conduct themselves in such a manner that they earn the trust and confidence of each other. The minorities must also realize that the religious feelings of the majority community are as sacred to them as their feeling are to them. They cannot bulldoze the majority community by their irresponsible behavior. We can't build Rome in a day; we can't reunite the broken hearts in a jiffy. We cannot heal centuries old wounds in days and months, we have miles to go, we cannot turn devils into saints overnight, and we cannot expect the victims of violence and injustice to forget everything so soon. But we have to give a wake up call for mental transformation.

Our Prime Ministers and several leaders have said many a time that we cannot change the neighbours. There cannot be two opinions about it but at the same time no one can dispute the assertion that we can change their hearts.

The book is free from any controversial statement, description, criticism or condemnation *qua* any individual, political party, group of people or religion/ faith. I believe that it is a unique academic venture to be appreciated by readers with non-jaundiced eyes.

It is a feather in my cap that Gyan Publishing House have agreed to publish my book in the spirit in which they had published the books of eminent authors like Justice Rajindar Sachar, kuldip Nayar, Subhash Kashyap, Asghar Ali Engineer and a host of such other eminent men of letters.

It is another feather in my cap that many dignitaries including Hon'ble the Vice-President of India Shri Hamid Ansari have sent their messages to me appreciating my humble piece of work.

Khwaja Abdul Muntaqim
H-3, Dharma Apartments,
2-I.P. Extn., Delhi-110092
E-mail: amkhwaja2007@yahoo.co.in

1

Hindu-Muslim Unity

Unity among different sections of people in a country is its real strength. If fanatic Hindus and Muslims continue to adhere to their stereo-type outlook— 'Hate... Hate... Hate', the yawning gulf between these two great communities of the world will get widened further and Hindu-Muslim unity will ever remain an elusive proposition and the Indian secularism of which we boast and feel proud of will fall prey to it. Thus, both the communities will continue to suffer in varying degrees. All of us may claim to be good persons but at the same time all of us cannot claim to be good citizens.

Aristotle had rightly said that it is not always the same thing to be a good man and a good citizen. There may be hundred reasons to hate each other but the balance shall always tilt in favour of innumerable reasons to love each other. The very purpose of life is to be happy and desire for peace and contentment. The more we care for the happiness and well-being of others and the more warm-hearted feelings we have for others, the greater is our own sense of happiness, well-being and contentment and it helps us in reposing faith and confidence in each other and removing mutual misunderstandings generally-based on unfounded grounds. Our priority should be to share each other's joys and grief and extend every possible help to the needy in our daily lives. If we cannot do it, we can at least desist from harming each other.

"Anyone, who does not love one's country and the nation or loves another country and its countrymen more than one's own country and the countrymen, is not a patriot in any sense of the term whatever or whichever the yardstick of patriotism may be and there cannot be any compromise on this issue."

Spirit of patriotism must come from within. It is not to be injected.

It can, however, be inculcated in those wandering in the grey area by taking corrective measures. Those developing anti-country feelings for whatever reasons are to be dealt with cautiously. 'Tooth for tooth and eye for eye approach is no solution'. In the first instance, efforts should be made to find out as to what are the factors that have dragged them to this thorny track..Whether they are doing so of their own..... Whether they are being misguided by some extremist groups? Whether they are playing in the hands of some outside agencies? Whether they are mentally deranged? Do they have any grievances against the State or any section of the people? As far as possible, reformative approach should be the first preference, because, in case of its failure the law will ultimately take its own course, and there is no escape for any one from its clutches.

Patriotism, as defined in all standard dictionaries of global repute, is love for and devotion to one's country.

A country has no meaning or identity without nation or its people and their culture. Adlai E. Stevenson, an American politician, noted for his intellectual demeanour, eloquent oratory, and promotion of liberal causes has beautifully described the concept of patriotism. According to him, "Patriotism is not an emotional outburst; it is a life-time dedication. It may, however, be noted here that loyalty to the country does not necessarily mean loyalty to the government." Mark Twain Samuel Langhorne Clemens, better known by his pen name **Mark Twain**, has also said: "Loyalty to country ALWAYS. Loyalty to government, when it deserves it. Those opposing corruption in government or raising their voice against injustice cannot be dubbed as disloyal to the State. As a matter of fact, they discharge the highest obligation of patriotism, provided their intentions are not malafide and they are doing so in public interest and not as a political gimmick." In this regard Barack Obama's words are an eye opener. To quote:

'Let us summon a new spirit of patriotism,
of responsibility, where each of us resolves
to pitch in and work harder and look over not
only ourselves, but each other.'

Sometimes there may be some confusion between 'patriotism' and 'nationalism'. George Orwell, a British man of letters, has rightly stated that nationalism is not to be confused with patriotism. According to him, 'patriotism' means devotion to a particular place and a particular way of life, which one believes to be the best in the world but has no wish to force on other people. The abiding purpose of every nationalist is to secure more power and more prestige, not for himself but for the nation or other unit in which he has chosen to sink his own individuality. As a matter of fact, both the terms are corollary to each other and they are so inter- linked and inter-woven that one cannot be separated from the other. Can one be a true nationalist without being a real patriot? Can one be a true patriot or real nationalist, who divides the nation or gets oneself indulged in anti-state activities? Those encouraging our cohesion as a nation should be supported and brought to power. Likewise, one must love and should have due regard for one's culture though it may be diverse because diversity of culture is its own beauty. This is the reason that we feel proud of our centuries old composite culture. Mohandas K. Gandhi, the Father of the Indian nation, had rightly said that culture lives in the hearts and in the soul of its people.

Past gives us a window into the future and it is very difficult to forget or ignore all painful events and episodes of the past, but what is ignorable or what creates division in the society or ill-will among various sections of the society should be ignored. **Can we change the history? "Learn to accept what you cannot change."**

- *The Ramayana* (Book 2).

Now, the ball is in the court of the social groups, clerics, politicians, intellectuals, human rights activists and all institutions and organisations that have been championing the cause of peace and harmony and can be instrumental in getting this objective accomplished. They cannot create a new world but they, by their sincere efforts, can bring about a change in the mind-set of the common man. All these groups can, undoubtedly, play a vital role in making their mission reachable to the common man because no mission can be successful without their participation. Intellectuals can show and lead to the right path but the path becomes a passage only when the people use it as thoroughfare. These groups through their writings, publicity material, and, above all, through their actions can impress upon and communicate to the people at large that **there is no religion in the world or there are no rules of ethics that do not speak of love, compassion, justice, freedom, peace, co-existence, honesty, liberty, dignity, fairness, mercy, tolerance, mutual respect, communal harmony, truth, non-violence and service to the society** and all these values flow from and are core essence of all religions and ethical norms and it is the people, may not be all, who have been practising contrary to what is contained in their religious scriptures or rules of ethics. They should sit together and draw up an agenda to make the message feasibly communicable so that it reaches the people and it ultimately becomes the voice of the people because *vox populi vox dei*, an Italian proverbial aphorism of common political wisdom, ultimately rules the scene.

The people must understand that religion is also a moral code and moral codes may differ. We should learn to live with a difference. It is not important whether the teachings of all religions are the same or not. These moral codes and beliefs should not divide the people. Oneness of all religions is a great idea and we, the Indians, have shown to the whole world that we have been its practitioners. But at the same time, it cannot be denied that the people have remained divided on these counts, too. Thus, it would be quite appropriate to evolve a new strategy and adopt a new approach to the whole problem. Instead of stressing the oneness, being not acceptable to all, we may directly address the differences and ask the people to accept them, live with them and not to make them an issue or a bone of contention. It is another pathway to achieve oneness because we have adhered to and religiously practised the principle of 'unity in diversity' for centuries together and the rich glorious heritage of India is not the heritage of any particular community; it is the common heritage shared by one and all.

Gandhi's Doctrine of Hindu-Muslim Unity

Hindu-Muslim unity is the need of the hour and it is as much needed today as it was about hundred years ago. An extract from Gandhi's article on Hindu-Muslim unity written in the first quarter of 20th century, reproduced below, bears testimony to it.

That unity is strength is not merely a copy-book maxim but a rule of life is in no case so clearly illustrated as in the problem of Hindu-Muslim unity. Divided we must fall....... Hindu-Muslim unity means not unity only between Hindus and Muslims, but between all those who believe India to be their home, no matter to what faith they belong.

"I am fully aware that we have not yet attained that unity to such an extent as to bear any strain. It is a daily-growing plant, as yet in delicate infancy, requiring special care and attention. The thing became clear in Nellore when the problem confronted me in a concrete shape. The relations between the two were none too happy. They fought only about two years ago over the question of playing music whilst passing mosques. I hold that we may not dignify every trifle into a matter of deep religious importance. Therefore, a Hindu may not insist on playing music whilst passing a mosque. He may not even quote precedents in his own or any other place for the sake of playing music. It is not a matter of vital importance for him to play music whilst passing a mosque. One can easily appreciate the Muslim sentiment of having solemn silence near a mosque the whole of the twenty-four hours. What is a non-essential to a Hindu may be an essential to a Muslim. And in all non-essential matters a Hindu must yield for the asking. It is criminal folly to quarrel over trivialities. The unity we desire will last only if we cultivate a yielding and a charitable disposition towards one another. The cow is as dear as life to a Hindu; the Muslim should, therefore, voluntarily accommodate his Hindu brother. Silence at his prayer is a precious thing for a Muslim. Every Hindu should voluntarily respect his Muslim brother's sentiment. This, however, is a counsel of perfection. There are nasty Hindus as there are nasty Muslims who would pick a quarrel for nothing.

I know that there is much too much distrust of one another as yet. Many Hindus distrust Muslims........ Such an attitude of mind betokens impotence on either's part. If not their nobility, their desire to live in peace would dictate a policy of mutual trust and forbearance. There is nothing in either religion to keep the two apart. The days of forcible conversion are gone. Save for the cow, Hindus can have no ground for quarrel with Muslims. The latter are under no religious obligation to slaughter a cow. The fact is we have never before now endeavoured to come together to adjust our differences and to live as friends bound to one another as children of the same sacred soil."

As mentioned above, Hindus and Muslims will have to forget or ignore all painful events and episodes of the past. How present generation is responsible for the follies committed by earlier generation or generations? No legal system has ever allowed punishment to 'A' for the wrong-doings of 'B'. It is very easy to give sermons but it is very difficult to bury the past. But there are many examples where victims of fanaticism have reconciled to the new situation with the passage of time. Here is an indicative example which may appear to be of little significance to an ordinary reader but the message it carries is of great significance for objective reading by neutral readers or the readers with non-jaundiced eyes. Satya Pal Anand, an eminent Urdu writer, and a Hindu gentleman whose father was brutally killed within his sight during 1947 riots, had, in an interview to *Urdu Duniya*, a monthly magazine of National Council for Promotion of Urdu Language, Ministry of Human Resource Development, Government of India (March 2013 Volume 15, Issue: 3), said that he, having joined the band of progressive writers and attended various national and international conferences, has transformed himself. He recites *Quran* and feels as if he is a Muslim. It does not mean that he has professed Islam. It reflects the changing bent of his mind or the new mind-set. Just note the greatness of this gentleman who, instead of peeping into the past, is taking India to new heights. I firmly believe that whatever he says, he means that. There are thousands of such examples otherwise it was practically impossible for crores of Indian Muslims to live in peace with their Hindu brothers in India after communal holocaust of 1947.

Hindu-Muslim unity can be achieved only through sincerity *sans* hypocrisy. *Adhocism* with any selfish motive, be it for any purpose whatsoever, can never bring these two groups of people closer. Any third power or mischievous elements in our own country may easily exploit the situation as we Hindus and Muslims (or say, in Gandhi's words, nasty Hindus and nasty Muslims) become ready to cut each other's throats even in slightly provocative situations which many a time are the offshoot of baseless rumours or conspiracies hatched just to divide further these already two divided communities. There are such elements in both the communities in India as also outside who cannot afford to see these two communities as closely united as the body and the skirt. These are the elements who put in best efforts, sometimes openly and most of the times clandestinely, to keep them apart. We may or may not accept that there are persons in both the communities who cannot put up with or relish the melodious voice of a *Muazzin* (one who chants the call to prayer from a minaret or tower of a mosque) even at a reasonable pitch of voice or *shankh-dhvani* (the sound of a conch-shell used by the Hindus for offering libations). Such persons, by whatever name we may call them, so-called fundamentalists (a term used in a very narrow sense), communalists, fanatics, extremists or orthodox class of people, are not acceptable to the civilised world because tolerance, love for each other, dignity, fairness, compassion, etc., are not only core essence of all religions but all these values are the integral part of the universally accepted human rights. The real problem is that whatever is mentioned or ordained in our holy books and religious scriptures or whatever values we value and cherish or whatever we preach we do not act upon them or in other words we do not practise whatever we preach.

Indian Muslims, being a minority, deserve fair and compassionate treatment at the hands of their elder brothers, the Hindus, as they preferred to stay in India, a secular state and did not migrate to Pakistan, a theocratic state. Those who did not migrate to Pakistan can broadly be classified into four categories:

(a) Those who rejected the two nation theory;

(b) Those who lived in the areas where communal riots did not take place during the partition;

(c) Those who were willing to stay in India even at the cost of their lives because of their love for and attachment with their homeland;

(d) Those who were quite ignorant and did not understand as to what was happening around them. They remained indifferent.

Maulana Abul Kalam Azad, the veteran Muslim Congress man, who was a staunch critic of Jinnah's two-nation theory, delivered a speech on October 23, 1947, that is, after three months of partition, which throws light on the pitiable condition of Muslims left in India and also contains a message for meeting out fair treatment to them, if read between the lines objectively. Full speech of this great leader at *Shahi Jama Masjid*, Delhi, is reproduced below:

Maulana Azad's Speech delivered at Grand Mosque, Delhi, October 23, 1947

My brethren,

You know what has brought me here today. This congregation at Shahjehan's historic mosque is not an unfamiliar sight for me. Here, I have addressed you on several previous occasions. Since then we have seen many ups and downs. At that time, instead of weariness, your faces reflected serenity, and your hearts, instead of misgivings, exuded confidence. The uneasiness on your faces and the desolation in your hearts that I see today, reminds me of the events of the past few years.

Do you remember? I hailed you, you cut off my tongue; I picked my pen, you severed my hand; I wanted to move forward, you broke off my legs; I tried to run, and you injured my back. When the bitter political games of the last seven years were at their peak, I tried to wake you up at every danger signal. You not only ignored my call but revived all the past traditions of neglect and denial. As a result, the same perils surround you today, whose onset had previously diverted you from the righteous path.

Today, mine is no more than an inert existence or a forlorn cry; I am an orphan in my own motherland. This does not mean that I feel trapped in the original choice that had made for myself, nor do I feel that there is no room left for my *ashiana* (nest). What it means is that my cloak is weary of your impudent grabbing hands. My sensitivities are injured, my heart is heavy. Think for one moment. What course did you adopt? Where have you reached, and where do you stand now? Haven't your senses become torpid? Aren't you living in a constant state of fear? This fear is your own creation, a fruit of your own deeds.

It was not long ago when I warned you that the two-nation theory was death-knell to a meaningful, dignified life; forsake it. I told you that the pillars upon which you were leaning would inevitably crumble. To all this you turned a deaf ear. You did not realise that, my brothers! I have always attempted to keep politics apart from personalities, thus avoiding those thorny valleys. That is why, some of my messages are often couched in allusions. The partition of India was a fundamental mistake. The manner in which religious differences were incited, inevitably, led to the devastation that we have seen with our own eyes. Unfortunately, we are still seeing it at some places.

There is no use recounting the events of the past seven years, nor will it serve any good. Yet, it must be stated that the debacle of Indian Muslims is the result of the colossal blunders committed by the Muslim League's misguided leadership. These consequences, however, were no surprise to me; I had anticipated them from the very start.

Now that Indian politics has taken a new direction, there is no place in it for the Muslim League. Now, the question is whether or not we are capable of constructive thinking. For this, I have invited the Muslim leaders of India to Delhi, during the second week of November.

The gloom cast upon your lives is momentary; I assure you we can be beaten by none save our own selves! I have always said, and I repeat it again today; eschew your indecisiveness, your mistrust, and stop your misdeeds. This unique triple-edged weapon is more lethal than the two-edged iron sword which inflicts fatal wounds, which I have heard of!

Just think about the life of escapism that you have opted for, in the sacred name of *Hejrat (migration)*. Get into the habit of exercising your own brains, and strengthening your own hearts. If you do so, only then will you realise how immature your decisions were.

Where are you going and why? Raise your eyes. The

minarets of Jama Masjid want to ask you a question. Where have you lost the glorious pages from your chronicles? Was it only yesterday that on the banks of the Jamuna, your caravans performed *wuzu* (ablution)? Today, you are afraid of living here! Remember, Delhi has been nurtured with your blood. Brothers! Create a basic change in yourselves. Today, your fear is misplaced as your jubilation was yesterday.

The words 'coward' and 'frenzy' cannot be spoken in the same breath as the word 'Muslim'. A true Muslim can be swayed neither by avarice nor apprehension. Don't get scared because a few faces have disappeared. The only reason they had herded you in a single-fold was to facilitate their own flight. Today, if they have jerked their hand free from yours, what does it matter? Make sure that they have not run away with your hearts. If your hearts are still in the right place, make them the abode of God. Some thirteen hundred years ago, through an Arab *ummi* (unlettered) prophet Muhammad (S), God proclaimed, "Those who place their faith in God and are firm in their belief, no fear for them nor any sorrow." Winds blow in and blow out: tempests may gather but all this is short-lived. The period of trial is about to end. Change yourselves as if you had never been in such an abject condition.

I am not used to altercation. Faced with your general indifference, however, I will repeat that the third force has departed, and along with it, its trappings of vanity. Whatever had to happen has happened. If your hearts have still not changed and your minds still have reservations, it is a different matter. But, if you want a change, then take your cue from history, and cast yourself in the new mould. Having completed a revolutionary phase, there still remain a few blank pages in the history of India. You can make yourselves worthy of filling those pages, provided you are willing.

Brothers! Keep up with the changes. Don't say, "We are not ready for the change." Get ready. Stars may have plummeted down but the sun is still shining. Borrow a few of its rays and sprinkle them in the dark caverns of your lives.

I do not ask you to seek certificates from the new echelons of power. I do not want you to lead a life of sycophancy as you did during the foreign rule. I want you to remind you that these bright etchings which you see all around you are relics of *qafilas* (caravans of the celebrities) of your fore-fathers. Do not forget them. Do not forsake them. Live like their worthy inheritors, and, rest assured, that if you do not wish to flee from this scene, nobody can make you flee. **Come, today let us pledge that this country is ours, we belong to it and any fundamental decisions about its destiny will remain incomplete without our consent. (Emphasis laid by the author).**

Today, you fear the earth's tremors; once you were virtually the earthquake itself. Today, you fear the darkness; once your existence was the epicenter of radiance. Clouds have poured dirty waters and you have hitched up your trousers. Those were none but your fore-fathers who not only plunged headlong into the seas, but trampled the mountains, laughed at the bolts of lightning, turned away the tornados, challenged the tempests and made them alter their course. It is a sure sign of a dying faith that those who had once grabbed the collars of emperors, are today, clutching their own throats. They have become oblivious of the existence of God as if they had never believed in Him.

Brothers! I do not have a new prescription for you. I have the same old prescription that was revealed to the greatest benefactor of mankind, the prescription of the Holy Quran: "Do not fear and do not grieve. If you possess true faith, you will gain the upper hand." The congregation is now at an end. What I had to say, I have said, briefly. Let me say once again, keep a grip on your senses. Learn to create your own surroundings, your own world. This is not a commodity that I can buy for you from the market-place. This can be bought only from the market-place of the heart, provided you can pay for it with the currency of good deeds.

"May God's grace be on you!"

Let Indian Muslims recollect the pledge the great Maulana had suggested to them "Come, today let us pledge that this country is ours, we belong to it and any fundamental decisions about its destiny will remain incomplete without our consent." and act upon the advice of Maulana Azad and the State as also the people of India should help them in marching ahead. It is never too late. They should do it in short time though the art is long but they have to press on. The people of India and the State should not forget this great son of India who fought for united India with full force and the power at his command. Sardar Patel, popularly known as the Iron Man of India, had also advised the people of India in a post-partition public address at Lucknow 'Let us all, who belong to India, swim or sink together.'

2

Stumbling Blocks in the Path of Hindu-Muslim Unity

Historical Backlash

Partition of India in 1947:Partition of India was the death of India's composite culture or, if described in the present-day terminology, it was the death of the then almost united civil society, followed by human massacre on both the sides in which more than a million people were killed, several millions displaced and many more cut off from their roots. Parents got separated from their children, friends lost their friends, and lovers lost their dear ones. For all Indians, partition was not only the logical outcome of Britain's policy of 'divide and rule', but it was also the geographical slaughter of the Indian dominion as its pious land was surgically divided. Even fauna and flora and rivers and streams were not spared. For supporters of Jinnah's two-nation theory and those demanding a separate homeland, that is, Pakistan, it was the fulfillment of their cherished desire and the recognition of their struggle to have their separate identity. For the Bangladeshis, then known as Bengalis, who were the frontline supporters of Pak movement, was a deceptive dawn that proved to be the prelude to their achievement of their own country named "Bangladesh" in 1971, a prediction by Maulana Azad, proved to be a reality. For the British, it was an economic compulsion as they were not in a position to afford the cost of ruling this country as they had suffered heavy losses in Second World War. For freedom fighters; it was the glorious result of their movement. For the rest of the world and the world history, it was one of the most important events of twentieth-century. For the international civil society, it was a badly managed shameful end of Britain's imperial rule in India that proved a tragic and horrible experience for the hundreds of thousands of Hindus, Sikhs and Muslims, who were killed in the communal holocaust and nearly 15 million having become refugees in their homeland. Even after the partition, over the past six decades India and Pakistan have been in a state of constant confrontation fighting several wars and indulging in day-to-day skirmishes.

Communal situation even before the partition was not so rosy, but it was not as thorny as it became after the partition. None can deny that the partition far from solving the communal problem in India, further aggravated the situation as a considerable number of Hindus, the majority community, was of the view that Indian Muslims were responsible for the partition of the country and that they betrayed them and got the country partitioned. Indian Muslims played an appreciable role in the freedom movement, may not be as unitedly and cohesively as their Hindu brothers did, but unfortunately the role of Muslims in India's freedom struggle has not been portrayed properly in history books. Many Muslim leaders including Ghulam Nabi Azad and office bearers of various Muslim organisations like Jamiat-Ulama-I-Hind as also Muslim intellectuals and their counterparts in the majority community have admitted in open and at various public fora time and again that Muslims were not behind others in the fight for independence but the facts have/had not been properly highlighted in history books and the text books. According to a report published in *Indian Express,* dated 29/4/2012 Jamiatul Ulema Hind (JUH) criticised the government for "ignoring" Muslims' contributions in India's freedom movements.

Speaking at a seminar on Maulana Mahmoodul Hasan of Deoband, who had planned an armed movement called "Reshmi Rumal movement" to oust the Britishers from India, JUH secretary general Maulana Mahmood Madani said that it was necessary to create awareness among the young generation about how various communities including Muslims had collectively fought for the nation's independence. Pointing out that the collective effort of Hindus and Muslims for independence was a 'national asset'. Paying tributes to Maulana Mahmoodul Hasan for his role in the movement, state Governor Kamla Beniwal said that Maulana Hasan fully supported Gandhiji in the movement.

The Ulema of Deoband, with resoluteness and trust in Allah, have always been not only in the foremost rank of those who have struggled in the movement for the independence of India, but they have also frequently been in the lead of this movement for independence; and if it is seen more thoughtfully and justly, they were the first persons, the pioneers, who initiated this idea. The warmth, vigour and catholicity which were created in this movement in fact are indebted to them. Most of these gentlemen raised the banner of revolt against the

English government, fought face to face with the English army and many of them passed a good part of their lives in jail. The fact is that the history of the independence movement of India is so mixed up with the history of the Ulema and religious personalities that it is now difficult to separate one from the other. Political decline had reduced Muslims to a state of helplessness and misery, distraction and anxiety; by the establishment of Darul-Uloom, Deoband, they received equanimity, composure and stability.

(www. Darululoom.com)

There is no cogent reason to ignore the contribution of Muslims in freedom movement as also Hindu-Muslim unity. Can we ignore personalities like Maulana Abul Kalam Azad, Maulana Hussain Ahmed Madani, Ali Brothers, Dr. Ansari, Hakim Ajmal Khan, Saifuddin Kichlu and a host of other people, besides Muslim poets like Allama Iqbal, the composer of Tarana-i-Hind, and Hali whose works speak of Hindu-Muslim unity. Even Sir Syed Ahmed Khan, the founder of Aligarh Muslim University, had in unequivocal terms pleaded for Hindu-Muslim unity and had great regard for the composite culture of India. This conviction is so revealed in his unforgettable observation:

"India is like a bride which has got two beautiful and lustrous eyes—Hindus and Muslims. If they quarrel against each other, that beautiful bride will become ugly."

—Sir Syed Ahmed Khan

Subsequent treatment of Hindus in Pakistan and their nominal emergence on the national scene, undoubtedly inferior to one given to Muslims in independent India, and attitude of some Muslims indicating their separatism from the majority community and the policy of some fundamental Hindu and Muslim organisations of keeping both the communities apart aggravated the situation and, at the same time, it was alleged and complained that Muslims were reluctant to join national mainstream though the real situation was that such an atmosphere was created to keep them confined to their ghettos otherwise who would not like to share the benefits of development and keep oneself away from the national mainstream.

The innocent Muslim masses in India continue to pay heavy price for the creation of Pakistan though a period of more than six decades has elapsed since partition and no one knows as to how long this sword will continue to hang over their heads. They continue to face the problems of security and identity even today. Some major and minor communal incidents continue to detranquilise the peace off and on. Barring casual diplomatic efforts to bring India and Pakistan closer, no sincere efforts have been made to achieve desired proximity because a positive effort is one that yields positive results. We may or may not deny that all agreements between India and Pakistan—Tashkent to Shimla and thereafter— were political rather diplomatic compulsions just to defuse the situation then prevailing. Besides, there are certain elements in both the countries who miss no opportunity to pollute the atmosphere on one pretext or the other. Let the political intelligentsia ponder over it. Let the defaulters be brought to book and exposed because people of these two countries can no longer tolerate this stalemate. **We cannot change the neighbours but we can change their hearts**. Instead of making more bombs and missiles and naming them after Hindu and

Muslim kings, both the countries must strive hard to achieve peace in the region. If the fanatics or hardliners in both the countries, that is, India and Pakistan, are under an illusion that the former can wipe out the latter from the world map or the latter may hoist the flag at Delhi's Red Fort, it is not possible in the present day civilised world.

It will not be out of place to quote a portion of **Report of Justice Raghubar Dayal Commission of Inquiry on Communal Disturbances in Ranchi and Hatia in Bihar during 22nd and 29th August, 1967** that has a bearing on historical backlash and is relevant even today:

"We are aware of the acute communal situations arising in the country for a number of years prior to the partition. They were considered to be the result of the policy of the British Government – the policy of divide and rule. The communal incidents then were mostly of local significance and took place on account of some alleged local grievances, generally connected with the playing of music before mosques at prayer time, obstruction caused to the passing of *Tazias* by the branches of the *Peepal* or other holy trees, cow sacrifices at the time of *Bakr-Id* especially and on any pretext which may have come handy at the time to create some trouble. The feeling of animosity engendered on the occasion was, at the most, between local residents and once the affair was over, the parties reverted to their old relationship which, on the whole, was cordial and friendly. There was nothing of mistrust between the two communities, however much agitated they might become on some particular issue at the instance of some interested parties. In essence, there was hardly anything of religion in the dispute, which gave rise to communal disturbances in those days and it was on this account mainly that the communal disturbances were attributed to the government policy of divide and rule. The partition of the country on the basis of the Hindus and Muslims forming two nations presumed a real difference of nationality between the two communities. But the creation of Pakistan did not and could not have removed most of the Muslim population of India to Pakistan. Whatever be the number of Indian Muslims who migrated to the newly created Pakistan, they must have been a very small proportion of the entire population. The Hindus naturally felt unhappy about the partition of the country and consequently felt a grievance against the Muslims whose attitude during the national struggle for independence, according to them, led to the partition of the country."

The commission, in its recommendations, has also mentioned that the root cause of the breaking out of serious disturbances as a result of any minor incident has been found to be the mistrust existing between the two communities since 1947 when the partition of the country took place. All efforts have to be made to remove this mistrust. What efforts should be is for the political and social parties to evolve. Genuine improvement of the relations between the two countries, Pakistan and India, may go a long way in allaying the apprehensions born out of mistrust and ultimately in removing the mistrust. ... The political parties should change their attitude in approaching the people for their damn, especially in elections. They should not exploit communal or caste feelings for their purposes. No political, economic or cultural issues should be discussed or agitated from a purely communal angle. Communal harmony should be taken to be too sacred to be tampered with for mere political gain..."

What the commission had stated more than 40 years ago may not be acceptable today in toto but no one can deny that it is still a debatable issue. As per PTI report of December 8, 2012, Press Council of India chief Markandey Katju, a retired Judge of the Supreme Court, holds the view that ninety percent of Indians can easily be misled by mischievous elements in the name of religion (*a view which may not be acceptable to many of us*). Justice Katju had also remarked that today 80 per cent of Hindus are communal and 80 per cent of Muslims are communal. He also said that this is the harsh truth, bitter truth and that in 150 years we have gone backwards instead of moving forward because the English kept injecting poison. The policy that emanated from London after the mutiny in 1857, that there is only one way to control this country, that is to make Hindus and Muslims fight each other. He also claimed that divisions had arisen from the language propaganda that decreed Hindi and Urdu to be the native tongues of Hindus and Muslims, respectively. He further added that the cause of the Kashmir problem is the partition of India on a totally bogus basis – the two-nation theory, that Hindus and Muslims are separate nations. Justice Katju justified his remarks as part of his intent to educate the Indian people, and explain the causes behind religious conflict in the country. One may or may not appreciate his observations, but no one can deny that communalism still persists in our country.

There are some elements in India who think even today that Muslims are still a threat and can make a come-back any time through means, fair or foul. The wholesale migration of the elite to Pakistan and the current social and economic conditions of Muslims, as so revealed in Sachar Committee Report and Ranganath Mishra Commission Report, are not any consolation to them and still it is a part of their hate campaign against Muslims.

Hindu distrust of Muslims and Muslim distrust of Hindus

Prof. P. Krishna, while delivering a lecture during the conference on peace and conflict held at the Indian Section Headquarters of the Theosophical Society, Varanasi, on 7th March, 2010, had dealt with this subject in the terminology understandable by the common man but it, unfortunately, does not reach them or certain vested interests do not want it to be reached. To quote:

"... if we really deeply want to understand an issue, we must not form opinions about it... To get to the root, one has to dig deep."

Each community feels 'we are different from them'. How does the mind define and draw that line? That is another fundamental question. Who are the 'we' and who are 'they'? On what basis does the mind draw that line? So is it just a matter of drawing a line on the earth or is the line here inside my head? On what basis does the mind draw that line? Were the people in Pakistan not our people before 1947, and we loved them as our brothers and today, because there is a line drawn across the nation by the British, they are no longer our brothers? That is another question we need to examine closely. When does a difference turn into a division and why? Difference is natural. We are all different from each other: in our age, in our wealth, in our knowledge, in our skin colour, in our size and shape. Is the division also a fact, or is it a creation of my own mind, my limited form of thinking?

Let us examine that question. Is the Hindu really very different from the Muslim? That is a very major source of conflict today in our country. I am taking that as an example. Are these two human beings really different in fact or they feel they are very different just because they think so? Thinking, can be changed. If they find that their thinking is false, it will end. Illusion can end through the perception of the truth. If you discover that the false is false and the truth is true, then the false ends. Therefore illusion can end. Therefore, if the cause is rooted in illusion, it can be eliminated, but when the cause is not rooted in illusion you can't eliminate it. So it is important to investigate that. So, I ask: Is the Hindu really different from the Muslim (or the Palestinian from the Jew) or they only think so? Let us examine it scientifically. Are their bodies very different? The medical scientist will tell you, "I can't tell from looking at the body or the contents of the body whether it is that of a Muslim or a Hindu". When he was born he was born in the same way. All this difference is imposed afterwards.

This whole national division comes about through identification. I identify myself with India and I feel Indian culture is superior to other cultures. Also, I feel only for these people and want to work only for them. Why? Why should I not read Shakespeare just because he was born in England or not read Lao Tsu because he was born in China? What has it to do with where a human being is born? Global mind feels for the whole of the earth and the whole of humanity. When the illusion ends, the narrowness in the mind ends...When the British came here, they looked down on the Indians because they ate with their hands and not with knife and fork. When the Indian goes there, he asks, why do these chaps have to eat with knife and fork when they have fingers? Both are just opinions arising from the fact that one man was taught that and the other man was taught something else. That is all. There is nothing superior or inferior about it. So does division arise when we attribute superiority or inferiority to a difference?

We do sometimes see a difference only as a difference. But when you see a man doing *Namaz* and you see another man praying in the temple you see more than just a difference and develop like and dislike. Why doesn't the mind perceive that also as just a difference?

In addition to that, Hindus and Muslims in India have been in close contact for centuries and so have had plenty of opportunity to clash. A lot of conflicts rise from the fact that India was first Hindu and then it was conquered by Muslims who established the Mughal empire, demolished Hindu temples and built mosques on Hindu holy sites. Another problem arose when the British rule of India was ending. The British, who were unhappy at being thrown out, decided to set the people against one another before they left. They raised tensions, and … a partition finally happened, that left both sides feeling sore and ill-treated. … Then the issue of Babri Masjid, an abandoned Muslim mosque [Never mind that it was not in service anymore].

For these and countless other reasons, there is some animosity between some Hindus and some Muslims. Also, the hatred depends on the individuals, not the community at large. Not all the Hindus hate Muslims, and not all the Muslims hate Hindus. Especially in India, Hindus and Muslims live in harmony now!"

Indeed, we need such Hindus and Muslims who believe in peace whole heartedly and are against retaliation, that is, eye for eye and tooth for tooth even in compelling situations. We can't hope for peace in the world until we have peace in our heart and display self-control even in provoking situations. Peace is the natural state of mind; it should not be allowed to be cut into pieces. Religious and spiritual leaders may preach and tell their followers, friends and foes as to how one can live in a world of differences without any fear and without imposing their ways or will on others.

Communal harmony cannot be achieved by fighting or finding fault with each other or criticising each other's religions. It can be achieved only through positive cooperation of all communities. Sometimes, it is said that the real source of communal violence and conflict within India lies outside India and that external forces who are opposed to the ideology of secularism obstruct us in implementing our secular agenda. Even if it is presumed to be correct, Indian Muslims are in no way responsible for that. Sometimes, it is also alleged that they get funds from other countries for fermenting communal hatred. Again, the answer is that the responsibility lies on the State. The State must curb such elements, if any, and take corrective measures. Good and bad are not to be treated at par. There should be an objective exercise to separate 'chaff from the grain' so that innocent people are not penalised and they are not subject to any inhuman and derogatory treatment and furthermore their human rights that are enshrined in the international covenants and the Constitution of India are not violated. At the same time, it is also equally important that all minorities, whether Muslims, Christians, Sikhs or Parsis, must not do anything that hurts the feelings of the majority community. Communal harmony is a reciprocal concept. Do good to others, only then they will do good to you. It is the constitutional duty of the majority and minority communities to conduct themselves in such a manner that they earn the trust and confidence of each other. The minorities must also realise that the religious feelings of the majority community are as sacred to them as their feeling are to them. They cannot bulldoze the majority community by their irresponsible behaviour.

Thus, the situation warrants that religion, which is a noble sentiment, should be used for a noble cause, that is, for striving to have a society in which everyone may live with dignity and honour and without discrimination in India. Everyone must respect and be taught to respect other religions. No one should utter or do anything which brings disrespect to the other religion. Mutual respect is the panacea for getting rid of communalism. The government should form a committee composed of liberal religious personalities to select the best things in each religion and recommend to the government to include them in the school curriculum so that the mind of our child student does not get polluted at the initial stage and he or she comes up with a feeling that all religions are good and there is no reason for hating anyone on ground of religion or belief. The message of communal harmony must also go to the people through mass media, print media, the electronic media, the film industry, the non-governmental organisations and such other agencies. There must be interaction amongst religious heads to sort out their differences, if any. Experience shows that anyone who tries to learn deeply from other religions, his own knowledge and understanding of his religion gets deepened and his approach becomes objective.

India has a long history of its composite culture. If a dispute arises among different communities, it may be settled amicably. No such problem can be solved if political leaders or those having other interests, say, economic, try to earn any mileage out of that[1].

Religion can never be the cause of communalism if the contents of religious scriptures and holy books of all religions are interpreted objectively and the policy of picking and choosing controversial matter without reference to the context and that, too, with ulterior motive by certain vested interest and persons with *malafide* intention is given up, sooner the better.

The Ayodhya Issue

India is a secular country and it is the home of several religions. Hindus, Muslims, Christians, Sikhs, Zoroastrians (Parsis), Buddhists, Jains, Jews, Jevovah's witnesses, etc., live in it as one people, the people of India.

One billion population of India consists of six main ethnic groups and 52 major tribes, six major religions and 6,400 castes and sub-castes; eighteen major languages and 1,600 minor languages and dialects. The essence of secularism in India can best be depicted if a relief map of India is made in mosaic, where the aforesaid one billion people are the small pieces of marble that go into the making of a map. Each person, whatever his/her language, casts, religion, has his/her individual identity, which has to be preserved, so that when pieced together it goes to form a depiction with the different geographical features in India. These small pieces of marble, in the form of human beings, which may individually be dissimilar to each other when placed together in systematic manner, produce the beautiful map of India. Each piece, like a citizen of India, plays an important part in making of the whole. The variations of the colours as well as different shades of the same colour in a map are the result of these small pieces of different shades and colours in marble, but even when one small piece of marble is removed, the whole map of India would be scarred, and the beauty would be lost. Each of the people of India has an important place in the formation of the nation. Each piece has to retain its own colour. By itself, it may be an insignificant stone, but when placed in a proper manner, it goes into the making of a full picture of India in all different colours and hues. A citizen of India stands in a similar position. The Constitution recognises the differences among the people of India, but it gives equal importance to each of them, their differences notwithstanding, for only then can there be a unified secular nation. Recognising the need for the preservation and retention of different pieces that go into the making of a whole nation, the Constitution, while maintaining, *inter alia*, the basic principle of equality, contains adequate provisions that ensure the preservation of these different pieces. The essence of secularism in India is the recognition and preservation of the different types of people, with diverse languages and different beliefs, and placing them together so as to form a whole and united India.[2]

In another case in, the Supreme Court of India[3] has propounded the positive concept of secularism in the following words:

"Pluralism is the keynote of Indian culture, and religious tolerance is the bedrock of Indian secularism. It is based on the belief that all religions are equally good and efficacious pathways to perform for God realisation.

It stands for a complex interpretative process in which there is a transcendence of religion and yet there is a unification of multiple religions. It is a bridge between religions in a multi-religious society to cross over the barriers of their diversity. Secularism is the basic feature of the Constitution as guiding principle of State policy and action. Secularism in the positive sense is the cornerstone of an egalitarian and forward looking society which our Constitution endeavours to establish. It is the only possible basis of uniform and durable national identity in a multi-religious and socially disintegrated society. It is a fruitful means for conflict resolution and harmonious and peaceful living. It provides a sense of security to the followers of all religions and ensures full civil liberties, constitutional rights and equal opportunities."

Despite such heart-touching rulings and that, too, of the Apex Court, whose rulings are binding on all courts within the territory of India under Article 141 of the Constitution, sometimes such things do happen that should not have happened in the traditional Indian society which has been accommodative and tolerant of various faiths or ways of life. Demolition of *Babri Masjid* is one such happening.

Ayodhya Issue is basically a religious issue to which both Hindus and Muslims are the aggrieved parties. Muslims are aggrieved because they feel that by demolition of Babri Masjid they have been deprived of their religious right to offer prayers in a mosque which is also a legal right for the disturbance of which a Muslim is entitled to seek relief in a court of law.[4] On the other hand, absolute majority of Hindus firmly believes that it is the birth place of Lord Rama and it is their cherished desire that Ram temple is constructed exactly at the same site. Even the most secular and moderate Hindus who are not anti Muslim and were not in favour of demolition of *Babri Masjid* earnestly desire that Ram temple should be constructed. They could be seen whispering in closed chambers but they do not express such feelings in open because of backlash from their community or because of their love for or proximity with Muslim community. It is a ground reality and no one can deny it and there cannot be two opinions about it.

A religious issue should preferably be resolved by the clergy as such a verdict will be well-received by both the parties, particularly in a country like India where we have still a religiously sensitive society. But our clergy, representing different communities, is also a divided lot. Political leanings and other factors have hit hard their mental faculties and deprived them of their objectivity. It, however, does not mean that such issue cannot be resolved by the courts. Judicial decisions have greatly affected the ambit of religious laws in the sub-continent as also globally extending the old principles to cover new cases or doubtful points by means of analogies and interpretations. The results of their untiring and ceaseless efforts are writ large on every page of law reports. But it has been noticed that in religious matters the emotions rise so high or are aroused to such an extent that even the most rational persons become irrational and fall prey to communal politics. Even orders of the courts are thrown to the winds. Many mosques have been demolished in partitioned/unpartitioned India as also in other parts of the world, including Pakistan and Saudi Arabia but *Babri Masjid* was demolished in peculiar circumstances and in a peculiar style:

1. *Babri Masjid* was demolished in a communally surcharged atmosphere and that, too, at a place which was only a few kilometers away from the Army Cantonment and the Army could be called immediately.

2. It was demolished in broad daylight in gross violation of the orders of the Supreme Court to maintain *status quo.*

3. It was demolished under the Chief Ministership of a person who had assured the Supreme Court that the *status quo* shall be maintained.

4. It continued to be demolished uninterrupted for hours together and the entire nation as also the world community continued to watch it on TV.

5. Demolition of *Babri Masjid* demolished the faith of the Muslim community, particularly the Muslim intellectuals, in Indian secularism, at least for the time being.

But time is a great healer. Sensitivity of the issue continued to be minimised with the passage of time, but it raises its ugly head or its ugly head "is raised" whenever the situation "so warrants". Thus, the situation warrants that this problem should be solved without further loss of time. Good opportunity should be availed of because it may pass away like the cloud.

It is the constitutional duty of the majority and minority communities to conduct themselves in such a responsible manner that they earn the trust and confidence of each other. As said earlier, the minorities must also realise that the religious feelings of the majority community are as sacred to them as their feelings are to them. This problem is to be solved in this spirit.

Generally, it is the elder brother (the Hindu community in this case) who gives concession to the younger one (the Muslim community), but here the expectation is just the reverse. The reason is obvious. Ayodhya is "Mecca" to the majority community. Thus, the only way out is that this matter be referred to the scholars of both schools of thought, that is Sunni and Shia schools with their seats at Deoband, Bareilly, Banaras, Lucknow, Calicut, etc., and their opinion sought.

They should put in best efforts to arrive at a consensus by bestowing their industrious learning and studied wisdom. Such an exercise is permissible under the Islamic jurisprudence. *Ijma* (general concord or concurrence) of *ulemas* (Islamic Scholars) is looked for the solution of all cases of doctrinal controversies. There is a tradition of the Prophet(S) in which he is said to have described *ulemas* as the heirs of the Prophet(S) on whom the mission of binding and loosing fell. There may be some differences of opinion as to the authenticity of these traditions between Sunni and Shia scholars, but both of them will agree that the instant issue deserves to be addressed rationally and resolved amicably in the larger interest of the society.

The solution may carry with it some concession by one party to the other, but any such concession from either side cannot/should not be described as surrender. It should be taken as the greatness of the giver and compulsion for the taker. Let both the communities behave like great people of a great country and march ahead to accomplish the unaccomplished national agenda. Can a civilised country or a nation afford further bloodshed on such an issue? Is it not unbecoming of a country aspiring to become a permanent member of the Security Council of the United Nations to afford further damage to the reputation of this secular state?

Still, we have miles to go.

Cow Slaughtering and Food Habits

Food is an important part of religious observance for all religions and faiths, including Hinduism, Christianity, Islam, Buddhism, Sikhism, Judaism, etc. Sometimes, even different types of food (vegetarian/non-vegetarian) and drinks (alcoholic and non-alcoholic) are served separately. Even non-vegetarian food (*Halal* and non-*Halal*) or meat of different animals like cow, goat, buffalo and pig are served separately because meat eaters also eat meat strictly according to their religious dictates. Sometimes, keeping in view religious sentiments of different communities, feasts are arranged on different days and different premises so that religious feelings of members of different communities do not get hurt.

Sanctity of Cow for Hindus : Hinduism is based on the concept of omnipresence of the Divine and the presence of a soul in all creatures. Thus, by that definition, killing or slaughtering any animal is a sin under Hinduism as one would be obstructing the natural cycle of birth and death of that creature, and the creature would have to be reborn in that same form because of its unnatural death.

The cow and bull are sacred to Hindus as they represent the symbol of *Dharma*. Beef is forbidden in the scriptures, and the bulls and cows are offered special protection by followers of the *Vedas*. Let Muslims appreciate it and refrain from quoting from religious scriptures and other literature pertaining to Hinduism to prove that cow slaughter or sacrifice of other animals corresponds exactly to such rituals in *Islam* even if some writers professing Hindu religion or any other religion support their point of view. It is not the command of law; it is an idea inherent in the principle or concept of peaceful co-existence. Such an exercise may create ill-will amongst these two major communities of India and the world. They (the Muslims) should follow religious dictate that is contained in the Holy Quran:

"To you be your way,

And to me mine."

The cow was also venerated by Mahatma Gandhi, the father of the Indian nation. His views regarding "Cow Protection" contained in the "Compilation of Views of Mahatma Gandhi on Cow Protection" (http://www.mkgandhi.org/momgbook/ Chap.81.html), are indicative of his love for the animal.

"THE COW is a poem of pity. One reads pity in the gentle animal. She is the mother to millions of Indian mankind. Protection of the cow means protection of the whole dumb creation of God. The ancient seer, whoever he was, began with the cow. The appeal of the lower order of creation is all the more forcible because it is speechless.[5]

...The cow is the purest type of sub-human life. She pleads before us on behalf of the whole of the sub-human species for justice to it at the hands of man, the first among all that lives. She seems to speak to us through her eyes: 'you are not appointed over us to kill us and eat our flesh or otherwise ill-treat us, but to be our friend and guardian'.[6]

I worship it and I shall defend its worship against the whole world.[7]

Mother cow is in many ways better than the mother who gave us birth. Our mother gives us milk for a couple of years and then expects us to serve her when we grow up. Mother cow expects from us nothing but grass and grain. Our mother often falls ill and expects service from us. Mother cow rarely falls ill. Here is an unbroken record of service which does not end with her death. Our mother, when she dies, means expenses of burial or cremation. Mother cow is as useful dead as when she is alive. We can make use of every part of her body—her flesh, her bones, her intestines, her horns and her skin. Well, I say this not to disparage the mother who gives us birth, but in order to show you the substantial reasons for my worshipping the cow.[8]

The Cow in Hinduism

The central fact of Hinduism is cow protection. Cow protection to me is one of the most wonderful phenomena in human evolution. It takes the human being beyond this species. The cow to me means the entire sub-human world. Man through the cow is enjoined to realise his identity with all that lives. Why the cow was selected for apotheosis is obvious to me. The cow was in India the best companion. She was the giver of plenty. Not only did she give milk, but she also made agriculture possible...

Cow protection is the gift of Hinduism to the world. And Hinduism will live so long as there are Hindus to protect the cow... Hindus will be judged not by their Tilaks, not by the correct chanting of Mantras, not by their pilgrimages, not by their most punctilious observances of caste rules, but their ability to protect the cow.[9]

I would not kill a human being for protection of a cow, as I will not kill a cow for saving a human life, be it ever so precious.[10]

My religion teaches me that I should by personal conduct instill into the minds of those who might hold different views, the conviction that cow-killing is a sin and that, therefore, it ought to be abandoned.[11]

Cow slaughter can never be stopped by law. Knowledge, education, and the spirit of kindliness towards her alone can put an end to it. It will not be possible to save those animals that are a burden on the land or, perhaps, even man if he is a burden.[12]

My ambition is no less than to see the principle of cow protection established throughout the world. But that requires that I should set my own house thoroughly in order first.[13]

Cow protection to me is not mere protection of the cow. It means protection of that lives and is helpless and weak in the world.[14]

But let me reiterate...that legislative prohibition is the smallest part of any programme of cow protection... People seem to think that, when a law is passed against any evil, it will die without any further effort. There never was a grosser self-deception. Legislation is intended and is effective against an ignorant or a small, evil-minded minority; but no legislation which is opposed by an intelligent and organised public opinion, or under cover of religion by a fanatical minority, can ever succeed. The more I study the question of cow protection, the stronger the conviction grows upon me that protection of the cow and her progeny can be attained only if there is continuous and sustained constructive effort along the lines suggested by me.[15]

Goseva

Preservation of cattle is a vital part of *Goseva*. It is a vital question for India . . . There is urgent need for deep study and the spirit of sacrifice. To amass money and dole out charity does not connote real business capacity. To know how to preserve cattle, to impart this knowledge to the millions, to live up to the ideal oneself, and to spend money on this endeavour is real business.[16]

In so far as the pure economic necessity of cow protection is concerned, it can be easily secured if the question was considered on that ground alone. In that event all the dry cattle, the cows who give less milk than their keep, and the aged and unfit cattle would be slaughtered without a second thought. This soulless economy has no place in India, although the inhabitants of this land of paradoxes may be, indeed are, guilty of many soulless acts.

Positive Measures

Then, how can the cow be saved without having to kill her off when she ceases to give the economic quantity of milk or when one becomes otherwise an uneconomic burden? The answer to the question can be summed up as follows:

1. By the Hindus performing their duty towards the cow and her progeny. If they did so, our cattle would be the pride of India and the world. The contrary is the case today.

2. By learning the science of cattle-breeding. Today there is perfect anarchy in this world.

3. By replacing the present cruel method of castration by the humane method practised in the West.

4. By thorough reform of the pinjrapoles [institutions for aged cows] of India which are today, as a rule, managed ignorantly and without any plan by men who do not know their work.

5. When these primary things are done, it will be found that the Muslims will, of their own accord, recognise the necessity, if only for the sake of their Hindu brethren, of not slaughtering cattle for beef or otherwise.

The reader will observe that behind the foregoing requirements lies one thing and that is *ahimsa*, otherwise known as universal compassion. If that supreme thing is realized, everything else becomes easy. Where there is *ahimsa*, there is infinite patience, inner calm, discrimination, self-sacrifice and true knowledge.[17]

From *Young India*, 7-7-1927

In Nepal, a Hindu majority country, cow is the national animal and slaughtering of cows and bulls is completely banned.

Hindus believe in the interdependence of life and most of them don't eat meat from animals or any focd that has involved the taking of life and are vegetarians. Most of the Hindus do not eat beef or beef products, because the cow is held to be sacred. However, dairy products including milk, butter and yoghurt may be eaten. They also avoid foods that may have caused pain to animals during manufacture. As regards *Vedas, Rig Veda* (10.87.16) specifically condemns beef consumption. The *Atharva Veda* (8.6.23) also specifically bans specific types of meat-eating. Why should anyone waste one's time and energy in searching the material contradicting such assertions? Even otherwise exception can never be the rule.

For vegetarian Hindus, vegetarianism, as is so said, is based on three principles, that is, *ahimsa* (non-violence), offer of "pure" (vegetarian) food to a deity and receive it back as *prasada* (in **Hinduism**, food and water offered to a deity during worship. It is believed that the deity partakes of and then returns the offering) and the conviction that non-vegetarian food is detrimental for the mind and for spiritual development. Sometimes, *Mahabharata's* maxim that "Non-violence is the highest duty and the highest teaching," is quoted in support thereof.

Non-vegetarian Hindus

There are many Hindu groups that have continued to abide by strict vegetarian diet even in modern times in all continents of the world but India cannot be described as a predominantly vegetarian country. Why should it be propagated? All of us know it. We also know that reasonable religious convictions, be they of majority community or minorities, deserve full respect. Like other religious communities, Hindus also avoid forbidden items of food.

Sanctity of Cow for Muslims

The cow is only among the permitted cattle for sacrifice and is not enjoined or even recommended for this purpose. Prof. Tahir Mahmood (with co-author Dr. Saif Mahmood), an eminent jurist, described as a storehouse of Islamic law by Justice VR Krishna Iyer, former Judge of the Supreme Court of India and an unparalleled example of jurisprudential scholarship, by

Salman Khurshid, has, in his book titled "*Muslim Law in India and Abroad*", expressed his views on the subject at pages 17 and 18 in the following words:

"The Constitution of India contains a Directive Principle of State Policy (Article 48) mandating the State to take measures for the protection of the cow and its progeny (in view of its sanctity in the Hindu religion, as acknowledged in a Supreme Court ruling). Laws banning cow slaughter are now in force in most parts of the country. Meat-traders in some parts of the country went to the courts alleging that the ban violated their fundamental right to freedom of trade and occupation under the Constitution and, to buttress their case, dragged religion into the matter—as in the past cow has been among the cattle used for *Qurbani* (ritual sacrifice) on the *Baqrid* festival .

The Supreme Court has examined the religious belief of the Muslims in this regard and upheld the validity of such prohibitory laws. The judicial stand does not conflict with any provision of Muslim religion as the cow is only among the permitted cattle for *Qurbani* and is not enjoined or even recommended for this purpose.[18] On the contrary, the Prophet had once reportedly warned his people that cow milk had medicinal properties but its flesh could cause disease.[19]

Moderation in all walks of life including food habits as also manners for eating is central to the Muslim way of life. In Islam, the concept of *Halal* – meaning 'lawful or permitted' – is applied to all areas of a person's life and includes regulations surrounding food. All *Halal* foods are allowed whereas all prohibited foods (and other aspects of life) are called *Haram*.

The list of *Haram* foods includes pork, alcohol and any products that contain emulsifiers made from animal fats, particularly margarines.

Gelatin made from pork or from any other animal that is not *Halal*. Hence forbidden is forbidden. The term '*Halal*' literally means legal, lawful, allowable, free, right, having religious sanction (opposed to *Haram*); slaughter of an animal suitable and lawful for Muslims to eat, as per rules prescribed by *Shariat* (the religious law of Muslims). The term '*Haram*' literally means unlawful, not allowed, forbidden, prohibited, illegitimate, having no religious sanction (opposed to *Halal*).

Is a Muslim allowed to eat food made or prepared by a Hindu?

Yes, according to *Fatwa* (a notification of the decision by the *Muftis* in respect of a particular case), issued by Darul Uloom Deoband, as long as the meat is *halal* and slaughtered in a *halal* way, a Muslim is allowed to eat it, irrespective of the person who cooks it, provided that he or she follows the general conditions of cleanliness and hygiene. In this context, views of Dr. Monzer Kahf, a prominent Muslim economist and counsellor, were also quoted. He had clearly stated that if the meat is *halal*, it does not matter who cooks it. We have many examples by the Prophet (peace and blessings be upon him) and the Companions (may Allah Almighty be pleased with them all) that they had at times non-Muslim and non Ahlul-Kitab servants and it is very likely that they cooked for them. The Qur'an only speaks about the slaughtering in a particular way. Who cooks or processes it does not matter. Only conditions of general cleanliness are required to be fulfilled.

As regards Darul Uloom Deoband's *fatwa* regarding cow slaughtering, its stand has been very reasonable. On the one hand, in reply to a question whether the act of those slaughtering cow secretly and eating it was Islamically lawful or unlawful, it had opined that in the light of the *Shariah*, eating meat of cow is permissible, but on the other hand, it has clearly stated that people of the States where cow slaughter is banned should avoid it as slaughtering cow and eating its meat stealthily is unsuitable and wrong.

(http://darululoom-deoband.com/english/index.htm)

Buddhism

Most of Buddhists choose to become vegetarian and avoid killing of animals. Like Hindus, Buddhists also believe that violence or pain inflicted on others will rebound on you and as such they prefer vegetarian lifestyle.

Christianity

Even different sects of Christianity like Roman Catholic, Orthodox and Protestant differ from one another in regulations governing food and drink. Some Catholic and Orthodox Christians observe several feast and fast days during the year. For example, they may fast or avoid meat on Fridays, during Lent or on Good Friday. Some eat fish instead. Some Christians don't drink alcohol. These include many members of the Salvation Army and other Protestant churches. Mormons and Seventh Day Adventists also avoid caffeinated and alcoholic beverages. Many Seventh Day Adventists don't eat meat or dairy products.

Judaism

As regards Jews, Kashrut refers to the laws pertaining to food in the Jewish religion. They take

Kosher, that is, permitted food. Pork and shell-fish are strictly forbidden.

Sikhism

Akal Takht (Central Body for Sikh Temporal Affairs) Final Ruling

The *Akal Takht* represents the final authority on controversial issues concerning the Sikh Panth (community or collective), and in this regard the issue of meat eating has been settled. The *Hukamnama* (edict or clarification) issued by *Akal Takht Jathedar* (head priest or head caretaker) Sadhu Singh Bhaura dated February 15, 1980 that Amritdhari Sikhs can eat meat as long as it is *Jhatka* meat and that eating meat does not go against the code of conduct (Kurehit) of the Sikhs. Thus, a Sikh cannot be excommunicated for eating meat. The internationally renowned Sikh preacher Giani Thakur Singh Ji, a student of Damdami Taksal, explains the tradition as follows:

"Nihang Singhs eat *Jhatka* meat because of their traditions. The Guru allowed this tradition of *Jhatka* to be practised within his army and by his soldiers; it was not for civilians to eat.

It is evident from the perusal of the details recorded above that the role of food is worth evaluating while dealing issues involving cultural and religious diversities. In multi-religious countries and countries engaged in production and import/export of leather, leather vendors mention the kind of leather used in their products on the labels. A Muslim would not purchase pigskin leather. Likewise, a Hindu could avoid cow leather, particularly those who are strictly vegetarians. They may prefer neutral leather. Judaism forbids wearing leather shoes on Yom Kippur and during mourning. Jainism strictly prohibits the use of leather, an animal product. Prohibited animal products tend to vary from one country or region and religion to the other.

Subjective Interpretation of Religious Scriptures and Holy Books

The words, phrases, and sentences of Quran are ordinarily to be understood in their natural, ordinary or popular and grammatical meaning and any subjective interpretation or any interpretation leading to absurdity must be avoided. For example, some of our Hindu brothers and sisters think that the word *Kafir* refers to them only and it is a word of contempt. It simply distinguishes between those who accept the faith and those who reject it. It is neither an abusive term nor an expression of condemnation.

Faith is a matter of personal conviction and as such anyone who rejects a particular religion, may be Islam, is not to be condemned, abused or persecuted for his faith or belief. Surah *Al-Kafirun* also gives a clear message that *Kafirs* (those rejecting faith) are to be treated decently and not persecuted or condemned. To quote:

1. Say: O ye

   That reject not that

2. I worship not that

   which ye worship

3. Nor will ye worship

   That which I worship.

4. And I will not worship

   That which ye have been

   Wont to worship

5. Nor will ye worship

   That which I worship.

6. To you be your Way,

   And to me mine.

The problem is that sometimes people interpret the word *Kafir* literally, that is, according to rule of literal interpretation which sometimes (as in the present case) leads to absurdity. This word, if used in a positive sense, may be the source of getting someone's favour, particularly the beloved. Read couplets of Mir, Ghalib, Majaz or even contemporary poets. They have used this word to describe the beauty of their love, such as, *kafir ada* (the beautiful style with a sensual invitation). Sometimes, we use the words like *kufran-i nemat* (ingratitude of a favour) and *kufr tutna* (an unexpected happening). Hence, the words *kafir or kufr* should not be taken as abusive terms and a cause rather pretext for retaliatory use of any objectionable term against the other community. Undoubtedly, little knowledge is a dangerous thing and one should keep oneself at a distance to avoid any imminent danger. Hindus and Muslims of the past were too large-hearted, liberal and lived in harmony and used these terms in their writings and day-to-day jokes with their Muslim friends and so the Muslims with their Hindu friends.

Sometimes, by way of propaganda or as a part of communal agenda, it is alleged that Islam teaches Muslims that non-Muslims, being infidels, should be killed. This allegation is a mere allegation. It is nowhere mentioned in Qur'an. It is quoted out of the context without quoting the proviso. If one lays one's hands on this holy book so maliciously or subjectively, one may also find the advice with the words "do not offer *Namaz* (prayers) or 'do not go to mosques'. These words are followed by a rider "if you are polluted or dirty." Thus, any extract from any holy book without reference to its context may give a wrong message. Even if there are some contradictions in assertions, may be for the followers of other religions, why should they lay their hands only on such parts. Views may be conflicting and contradictory. In such situations, principle of harmonious construction which is generally applied for interpretation of statutes should be applied. It is a cardinal rule of construction that when there are two provisions which are in conflict with each other such that both of them cannot stand, they should, if possible, be so interpreted that effect can be given to both, and that a construction which renders either of them inoperative and useless should not be adopted except in the last resort.

The Muslims must also display by their conduct a correct understanding of Islamic concepts. Dr. Tahir Mahmood had also made a similar appeal to the Muslim community in early eighties. To quote:

"At a seminar held on 18th October, 1980 under the auspices of the Department of Islamic and Comparative Law, Indian Institute of Islamic Studies, New Delhi, he made an appeal to the Muslim community to display by their conduct a correct understanding of Islamic concepts..."[20]

References

1. *Protection of Human Rights (National and International Perspectives)* by Khwaja Abdul Muntaqim pp. 98, 99- Publishers: Law Publishers (India) Pvt. Ltd., Allahabad.

2. *Protection of Human Rights (National and International Perspectives)* by Khwaja Abdul Muntaqim pp. 98, 99- Publishers: Law Publishers (India) Pvt. Ltd., Allahabad).

3. Valsamma Paul v. Cochin University ((1996) 3 SCC 545).

4. *Pathanamthitta Majilissae Islamia v. Nagoor Meran Sheikh Muhammad A.I.R 1963 Kerala 49 at p. 51.*

5. (*YI*, 6-10-1921, p. 36).

6. (*YI*, 26-6-1924, p. 214).

7. (*YI*, 1-1-1925, p. 8).

8. (*H*, 15-9-1940, p. 281).

9. (*YI*, 6-10-1921, p. 36).

10. (*YI*, 18-5-1921, p. 156).

11. (*YI*, 29-1-1925, p. 38).

12. (*H*, 15-9-1946, p. 310).

13. (*YI*, 29-1-1925, p. 38).

14. (*YI*, 7-5-1925, p. 160).

15. (*YI*, 7-7-1927, p. 219).

16. (*H*, 17-2-1946, p. 11).

17. (*H*, 31-8-1947, p. 300).

18. Mohd Hanif Qureshi v State of Bihar AIR 1958 SC 731.

19. State of West Bengal v Ashutosh Lahiri AIR 1995 SC 464".

20. (*Islamic and Comparative Law Quarterly*, April-June 1981, p. 146).

3

Are Muslims Treated as Untouchables in India?

The answer is, constitutionally and legally, "NO". Untouchability has been abolished by Article 17 of the Constitution of India which reads as under:

"**17. Abolition of Untouchability**—"Untouchability" is abolished and its practice in any form is forbidden. The enforcement of any disability arising out of "Untouchability" shall be an offence punishable in accordance with law."

But it may not be wrong to say that still there are certain elements in our country who, what to talk of Muslims, consider even *Dalit* Hindus as untouchables and they are not allowed to enter certain temples and many a such case have come before various courts in India. However, according to the report, submitted by a government appointed committee led by a former Chief Justice of Delhi High Court, Rajindar Sachar, Muslims were now worse off than the *Dalits* who were called and treated as untouchables earlier and now called Scheduled Caste and Scheduled Tribe. Some 52 per cent of Muslim men were unemployed, compared with 47 per cent of *Dalit* men. Among Muslim women, 91 per cent were unemployed, compared with 77 per cent of *Dalit* women. Almost half of Muslims over the age of 46 couldn't read or write. While making up 11 per cent of the population, Muslims accounted for 40 per cent of India's prison population. Meanwhile, they held less than five per cent of government jobs. (For authentic statistical information census figures indicating socio-economic condition of various communities and groups of people may be referred).

On the other hand, India with 85 per cent Hindu population had three Muslim Presidents, high ranking military officers like Air Chief Marshal, several Chief Justices of India, besides great statesmen, top Bollywood stars, singers, artists, cricketers, poets, writers, etc., and all important Muslim shrines are being maintained by the government or being maintained under its supervision directly or indirectly But in contrast, we do not find such strong identical examples in the Muslim world, particularly countries with considerable Hindu population like Pakistan and Bangladesh.

Photographs:

Dr. APJ Abdul Kalam (born - 1931)

Term of Office: July 25, 2007 - July 25, 2012

Dr. Fakhruddin Ali Ahmed (1905-1977)

Term of Office: August 24, 1974 - February 11, 1977

Dr. Zakir Hussain (1897-1969)

Term of Office: May 13, 1967 - May 3, 1969

Ours is a typical country and a typical nation. On the one hand, sky is the limit for Muslims in India and they can reach any heights in any walk of life. On the other, we have a checkered history of communal violence in which Muslims have by and large been at the receiving end. Again, on the one hand, we have this communal history, but on the other, we have not extended our borders in the rich history of thousands of years. **Hindus and Muslims lived and co-existed in India for centuries. Why irrelevant questions, like whether they are Indians first or Muslims first, are put to them? Our Supreme Court has said in TMA Pai's case (J.T.2002(9)SC1) that our country is often depicted as a person in the form of "BHARAT MATA - MOTHER INDIA". The people of India are regarded as her children. Would it be advisable to ask its children whether they are children of their father first or their mother first? When all Indians are the children of "BHARAT MATA - MOTHER INDIA" why this question is put to Muslims only?** Many intellectuals belonging to different countries have also posed this question before various fora. Chennai-based freelance journalist Syed Ali Mujtaba, in his article captioned 'Indian Republic at 60', posted on January 29, 2010 has beautifully answered this question by stating that the answer is both. "I am born in India and I am an Indian and it is a geographical term. I am born in Islamic faith and so I am a Muslim, and it is a religious term. I am an "Indian Muslim" is the short answer."

Whenever we are in India, we may introduce or consider ourselves as Hindus, Muslims, Tamilians, Bengalis, etc., but when we are out of India we always introduce ourselves as Indians. The above-named journalist has put the same thing almost in the same terminology. To quote:

"My take on this is, to retort back; are you a Hindu first, or a *Brahmin* first, or an Indian first? If you move to Australia will you be a Hindu first, a Brahmin first, an Indian first or an Australian first?" How does a Hindu and an Indian reconcile to one's religious and national identity if he or she is not living in the geographical boundary of India?"

Why American Hindus of Indian origin support Sania Mirza in a match against American players? One can never, particularly up to two or three generations, ignore or forget his/her origin. Any other approach would be a mere philosophical proposition. These are the natural instincts. Even UNDECLARATION ON THE RIGHTS OF PERSONS BELONGING TO NATIONAL AND ETHNIC, RELIGIOUS AND LINGUISTIC MINORITIES, 1992 while appreciating such human tendencies has clearly recognised these rights in unequivocal terms. To quote:

Article 1

1. States shall protect the existence and the national or ethnic, cultural, religious and linguistic identity of minorities within their respective territories and shall encourage conditions for the promotion of that identity.

2. States shall adopt appropriate legislative and other measures to achieve those ends.

Article 2

1. Persons belonging to national or ethnic, religious and linguistic minorities (hereinafter referred to as persons belonging to minorities) have the right to enjoy their own culture, to profess and practice their

own religion, and to use their own language, in private and in public, freely and without interference or any form of discrimination.

2. Persons belonging to minorities have the right to participate effectively in cultural, religious, social, economic and public life.

3. Persons belonging to minorities have the right to participate effectively in decisions on the national and, where appropriate, regional level concerning the minority to which they belong or the regions in which they live, in a manner not incompatible with national legislation.

4. Persons belonging to minorities have the right to establish and maintain their own associations.

5. Persons belonging to minorities have the right to establish and maintain, without any discrimination, free and peaceful contacts with other members of their group and with persons belonging to other minorities, as well as contacts across frontiers with citizens of other States to whom they are related by national or ethnic, religious or linguistic ties.

Article 3

1. Persons belonging to minorities may exercise their rights, including those set-forth in the present Declaration, individually as well as in community with other members of their group, without any discrimination.

2. No disadvantage shall result for any person belonging to a minority as the consequence of the exercise or non-exercise of the rights set-forth in the present Declaration.

Article 4

1. States shall take measures where required to ensure that persons belonging to minorities may exercise fully and effectively all their human rights and fundamental freedoms without any discrimination and in full equality before the law.

2. States shall take measures to create favourable conditions to enable persons belonging to minorities to express their characteristics and to develop their culture, language, religion, traditions and customs, except where specific practices are in violation of national law and contrary to international standards.

3. States should take appropriate measures so that, wherever possible, persons belonging to minorities may have adequate opportunities to learn their mother tongue or to have instruction in their mother tongue.

4. States should, where appropriate, take measures in the field of education, in order to encourage knowledge of the history, traditions, language and culture of the minorities existing within their territory. Persons belonging to minorities should have adequate opportunities to gain knowledge of the society as a whole.

5. States should consider appropriate measures so that persons belonging to minorities may participate fully in the economic progress and development in their country.

Article 5

1. National policies and programmes shall be planned and implemented with due regard for the legitimate interests of persons belonging to minorities.

2. Programmes of cooperation and assistance among States should be planned and implemented with due regard for the legitimate interests of persons belonging to minorities.

Article 6

States should cooperate on questions relating to persons belonging to minorities, *inter alia*, exchanging information and experiences, in order to promote mutual understanding and confidence.

Article 7

States should cooperate in order to promote respect for the rights set-forth in the present Declaration.

Article 8

1. Nothing in the present Declaration shall prevent the fulfillment of international obligations of States in relation to persons belonging to minorities. In particular, States shall fulfill in good faith the obligations and commitments they have assumed under international treaties and agreements to which they are parties.

2. The exercise of the rights set-forth in the present Declaration shall not prejudice the enjoyment by all persons of universally recognised human rights and fundamental freedoms.

3. Measures taken by States to ensure the effective enjoyment of the rights set-forth in the present Declaration shall not *prima facie* be considered contrary to the principle of equality contained in the Universal Declaration of Human Rights.

4. Nothing in the present Declaration may be construed as permitting any activity contrary to the purposes

and principles of the United Nations, including sovereign equality, territorial integrity and political independence of States.

Article 9

The specialised agencies and other organisations of the United Nations system shall contribute to the full realisation of the rights and principles set-forth in the present Declaration, within their respective fields of competence.

Besides, **UN Declaration on the Elimination of All Forms of Intolerance and Discrimination Based on Religion** contains certain provisions which may be good reading material for readers in a multi-religious, multi-lingual and multi-cultural society like ours.

Article 1

Everyone shall have the right to freedom of thought, conscience and religion. This right shall include freedom to have a religion or whatever belief of his choice, and freedom, either individually or in community with others and in public or private, to manifest his religion or belief in worship, observance, practices and teaching.

No one shall be subject to coercion which would impair his freedom to have a religion or belief of his choice.

Freedom to manifest one's religion or beliefs may be subject only to such limitations as are prescribed by law and are necessary to protect public safety, order, health or morals or the fundamental rights and freedoms of others.

Article 2

No one shall be subject to discrimination by any State, institution, group of persons, or person on grounds of religion or other beliefs.

For the purposes of the present Declaration, the expression "intolerance and discrimination based on religion or belief" means any distinction, exclusion, restriction or preference-based on religion or belief and having as its purpose or as its effect nullification or impairment of the recognition, enjoyment or exercise of human rights and fundamental freedoms on an equal basis.

Article 3

Discrimination between human beings on grounds of religion or belief constitutes an affront to human dignity and a disavowal of the principles of the Charter of the United Nations, and shall be condemned as a violation of the human rights and fundamental freedoms proclaimed in the Universal Declaration of Human Rights and enunciated in detail in the International Covenants on Human Rights, and as an obstacle to friendly and peaceful relations between nations.

Article 4

All States shall take effective measures to prevent and eliminate discrimination on the grounds of religion or belief in the recognition, exercise and enjoyment of human rights and fundamental freedoms in all fields of civil, economic, political, social and cultural life.

All States shall make all efforts to enact or rescind legislation where necessary to prohibit any such discrimination, and to take all appropriate measures to combat intolerance on the grounds of religion or other beliefs in this matter.

Article 5

The parents or, as the case may be, the legal guardians of the child have the right to organise the life within the family in accordance with their religion or belief and bearing in mind the moral education in which they believe the child should be brought up.

Every child shall enjoy the right to have access to education in the matter of religion or belief in accordance with the wishes of his parents or, as the case may be, legal guardians, and shall not be compelled to receive teaching on religion or belief against the wishes of his parents or legal guardians, the best interests of the child being the guiding principle.

The child shall be protected from any form of discrimination on the ground of religion or belief. He shall be brought up in a spirit of understanding, tolerance, friendship among peoples, peace and universal brotherhood, respect for freedom of religion or belief of others, and in full consciousness that his energy and talents should be devoted to the service of his fellow men.

In the case of a child who is not under the care either of his parents or of legal guardians, due account shall be taken of their expressed wishes or of any other proof of their wishes in the matter of religion or belief, the best interests of the child being the guiding principle.

Practices of a religion or beliefs in which a child is brought up must not be injurious to his physical or mental health or to his full development, taking into account article 1, paragraph 3, of the present Declaration.

Article 6

In accordance with article 1 of the present Declaration and subject to the provisions of article 1, paragraph three, the right freedom of thought, conscience, religion or belief shall include, *inter alia*, the following freedoms:

(a) To worship or assemble in connection with a religion or belief, and to establish and maintain places for these purposes;

(b) To establish and maintain appropriate charitable or humanitarian institutions;

(c) To make, acquire and use to an adequate extent the necessary articles and materials related to the rites or customs of a religion or belief;

(d) To write, issue and disseminate relevant publications in these areas;

(e) To teach a religion or belief in places suitable for these purposes;

(f) To solicit and receive voluntary financial and other contributions from individuals and institutions;

(g) To train, appoint, elect or designate by succession appropriate leaders called for by the requirements and standards of any religion or belief;

(h) To observe days of rest and to celebrate holidays and ceremonies in accordance with the precepts of one's religion or belief; and

(i) To establish and maintain communications with individuals and communities in matters of religion and belief at the national and international levels.

Article 7

The rights and freedoms set-forth in the present Declaration shall be accorded in national legislation in such a manner that everyone shall be able to avail himself of such rights and freedoms in practice.

Article 8

Nothing in the present Declaration shall be construed as restricting or derogating from any right defined in the Universal Declaration of Human Rights and the International Covenants on Human Rights.

It will not be out of place to mention here that the Constitution of India does not lack in any of the areas mentioned in these UN documents and Indian Muslims are living in a country where they are enjoying complete religious freedom and anyone violating this freedom is punishable under law. Another special feature of this freedom is that all *maslaks* (schools of thought) are at liberty to perform their rituals in the way they like, a freedom not available even in some theocratic Islamic states. It should, however, be remembered that freedom of religion is sacrosanct but not absolute in the sense that individuals have responsibilities in exercising the right. This right is not to be exercised in such a way that it becomes nuisance for others.

Thus all of us must enjoy and let others enjoy this freedom and avoid entering into unnecessary controversies. Let us first learn to give love to our fellow beings irrespective of their class, creed, religion or origin and then teach them the basics of religion and patriotism. A true patriot is one who loves one's countrymen irrespective of their class, creed, religion or origin. Preamble to the Constitution of India begins with the words "WE THE PEOPLE OF INDIA..." It does not use the words "I and you". Anyone who hates any class of his countrymen or considers them as untouchables or behaves as such, or loves any other country more than one's own country is, undoubtedly, not an Indian first. Let my countrymen realise that ill-will against any class of people is an assault on its integrity as also the integrity of the country and the nation. Any bloodshed in the name of religion, and more so its glorification, is the greatest crime against humanity. They must understand that a match stick burns itself first before burning others. Such tendencies create chaos and disorder in the country. If we keep ourselves away from the national mainstream or certain elements do not allow any class of people to join national mainstream, self-pitying is the only course available to them. **There is a verse in *Bhagwad Geeta* which says "One should lift oneself by oneself and never fall into self-pitying oneself".** Life is a great opportunity for the man to achieve his highest potential; it should not fall prey to one's narrow outlook and thus be not thrown to dogs.

4

Both Hinduism and Islam are Religions of Peace: The Hindu and Muslim Perspectives

Certain groups of extremist Hindus, may be microscopic in nature, feel that they welcomed the Muslims with open arms as brothers but, in turn, Islam destroyed and decimated the entire Hindu civilisation and that the Muslims contributed nothing to the Indian culture, intellectual establishment or civilisation. While addressing Muslims they say, "You (Muslims) say your religion is a religion of peace but your religion teaches Muslims that non-Muslims are infidels and the highest religious leaders in your religion themselves use religious doctrine to justify killings." On the other hand, some other reputed writers feel otherwise and have opined as under:

Mahatma Gandhi
(*The Mind of Gandhi*, p. 100 by R.K. Prabhu and V.R. Rao)

Gandhiji writes: "Islam's distinctive contribution to India's national culture is its unadulterated belief in

Oneness of God and a practical application to the truth of brotherhood of man for those who are nominally within its fold."

Pandit Jawaharlal Nehru

(*The Discovery of India*, 1946, pp. 218, 225)

"The coming of Islam and of a considerable number of people from outside with different ways of living and thought affected these beliefs and structure. A foreign conquest, with all its evils, has one advantage: it widens the mental horizon of the people and compels them to look out of their shells. They realise that the world is a much bigger and a more variegated place than they had imagined. So, the Afghan conquest had affected India and many changes had taken place. Even more so the *Mughals*, who were far more cultured and advanced in the ways of living than the Afghans, brought changes to India. In particular, they introduced the refinements for which Iran was famous."

N.S. Mehta

'Islam and the Indian Civilisation,' reproduced in *'Hindustan ke Ahd-i-Wusta ki ek Jhalak,'* by S.A. Rahman)

"Islam had brought to India a luminous torch which rescued humanity from darkness at a time when old civilizations were on the decline and lofty moral ideals had got reduced to empty intellectual concepts. As in other lands, so in India too, the conquests of Islam were more widespread in the world of thought than in the world of politics. Today, also, the Islamic world is a spiritual brotherhood which is held together by community of faith in the Oneness of God and human equality. Unfortunately, the history of Islam in this country remained tied up for centuries with that of government with the result that a veil was cast over its true spirit, and its fruits and blessings were hidden from the popular eye."

Dr. Pattabhi Sitaramayya

(Presidential Address to the Fifty-fifth Session of the Indian National Congress, Jaipur, 1948)

"(The Muslims had) enriched our culture, strengthened our administration, and brought near distant parts of the country... It (the Muslim period) touched deeply the social life and the literature of the land."

Humayun Kabir

(*The Indian Heritage*, 1955, p. 153)

"Islam's democratic challenge has perhaps never been equalled by any other religious or social system. Its advent on the Indian scene was marked by a profound stirring of consciousness. It modified the basis of Hindu social structure throughout northern India."

Hinduism - the Religion of Peace and Non-violence

Hinduism, like other religions of the world, does not speak of hatred against any other religion. Its scriptures speak of non-injury, non-violence, tolerance, peace, compassion, and love towards all creatures. It speaks of *ahimsa*. In Sanskrit, the term "*Ahimsa*" means abstaining from causing hurt or harm to anyone. Even otherwise violence or any violent act is the most extreme form of wrong doing and is a clear deviation from the right path, the path of righteousness. The following quotations from various scriptures and holy books, being self-explanatory in nature, bear testimony to it:

To the heavens be peace, to the sky and the earth; to the waters be peace, to plants and all trees; to the gods be peace, to Brahman be peace, to all men be peace, again and again—peace also to me! —*Shukla Yajur Veda,* 36.17

If we have injured space, the earth or heaven, or if we have offended mother or father, from that may *Agni*, fire of the house, absolve us and guide us safely to the world of goodness. —*Atharva Veda,* 6.120.1

Protect both our species, two-legged and four-legged. Both food and water for their needs supply. May they with us increase in stature and strength? Save us from hurt all our days, O Powers! — *Rig Veda,* 10.37.11

When mind stuff is firmly based in waves of *ahimsa* all living beings cease their enmity in the presence of such a person. —*Yoga Sutra,* 2.35

O earthen vessel, strengthen me. May all beings regard me with friendly eyes! May I look upon all creatures with friendly eyes! With a friend's eye may we regard each other! —*Shukla Yajur Veda,* 36.18

He who sees that the Lord of all is ever the same in all that is—immortal in the field of mortality—he sees the truth. And when a man sees that the God in himself is the same God in all that is, he hurts not himself by hurting others. Then he goes, indeed, to the highest path.

—*Bhagavad Gita,* 13.27-28

"Here they say that a person consists of desires. And as is his desire, so is his will. And as is his will, so is his deed; and whatever deed he does, that he will reap."

—*The Brihadaranyaka Upanishad* (IV, 4, ii, 6)

"All suffering recoils on the wrong-doer himself. Therefore, those who desire not to suffer refrain from causing others pain."

— *Tiruvalluvar*

Like Hinduism, Buddhism and Jainism have also been teaching non-injury, called *ahimsa*, as a spiritual principle and practical ethic. The principles of *Dharma*, or divine law, as mentioned in Hindu scriptures, knew full well the potential for human suffering and the ways that could avert it and that spiritual power flowed in and through all things in this universe, animate and inanimate, conferring existence by its presence. According to John T. Platts, the compiler of "*A Dictionary of Urdu, Classical Hindi and English*", the term *Dharma* means-which is to be held fast or kept, religious observances, piety, prescribed course of conduct, duty, obligation, right, justice, equity, virtue, morality, morals, etc. Thus the practice of non-injury and non-violence is the ancient commitment of Hinduism.

Islam—The Religion of Peace

Each religion is the religion of peace and so Islam is, but, unfortunately, Islam is being presented as the religion of fanatics, barbarians and terrorists for no cogent reasons. Much has been said, alleged, propagated, preached and practised against Islam, Islamic tenets and Muslims, particularly in the recent past. Those indulged in such practices are either ill-informed, misinformed or biased.

Islam is a religion that lives not for itself but for the whole of humankind. In Islam, life of human being or any other creature is considered to be the most precious and valuable possession of the living being. It is clearly ordained in Holy Quran that he who kills a human being unjustly has not murdered only an individual but has killed that social self which is essence of humanity. But Muslims have failed to present their case before the world community, may be because of their poor advocacy or party at the other end being biased or non-receptive and a few wrong-doers have brought disgrace to the whole community. **Islam is not necessarily one what**

a functional Muslim does; Islam is one what a true Muslim should do.

Let the Muslims tell the whole world that they afforded both shelter and protection to Jews and Nestorians when they were being persecuted and massacred in various parts of the world.

Let the Muslims tell the whole world that Quran asked Muslims to do justice even to those who hate them and a few evil-doers cannot bulldoze the entire community.

Islam's Big "No" to Terrorism

Human rights are the essence of human life and it is the core essence of every religion that no human being should be subjected to cruel, inhuman or degrading treatment. No one has a right to do any violence to anyone's right to life, liberty and security of person. The UN charter also speaks of the determination of the peoples of the United Nations to reaffirm faith in fundamental rights, in the dignity and worth of human person. Thus, there is no sanction, be it religious or otherwise, for any act of violence, such as assault on innocent people, attack on the democratic institutions or economic nerve centres of any country, kidnapping, abduction, hijacking, piracy or militancy of any kind whatsoever. Howard Zinn, a former professor of Boston University, has rightly said that there is no flag large enough to cover the shame of killing innocent people.

The concern of the international community regarding terrorism is not new, Muslims are not its originators and its beginning cannot be attributed to the hijacking of TWA flight 847, crashing of an Air India Boeing 747, explosions at the Tokyo and Frankfurt, hijacking of Indian aircrafts to Pakistan and Afghanistan airports, followed by recent incidents like terrorist attacks in New York, Washington D.C. and Pennsylvania on September 11, 2001 and further followed by attacks on Indian Parliament, Jammu and Kashmir Assembly, and Mumbai and more recently brutal killing of Indian soldiers etc.

After the assassination of King Alexander of Yugoslavia and the Foreign Minister of France by a "foreign hand" in Marseilles "On French soil" in 1934, the League of Nations sponsored a Convention for the Prevention and Punishment of Terrorism on 16 November 1937.[1]

Any act of violence should not be attributed to the religion of the person committing it. If such a subjective approach is adopted, all religions shall be deemed to be the religions professed by the terrorists and the perpetrators of violence. Assassin of Mahatma Gandhi was a Hindu, whereas killer of Anwar Sada'at was a Muslim. Likewise, Abraham Lincoln fell to the bullet of a Christian and Mrs. Indira Gandhi was shot dead by a Sikh. Does it mean that all these religions do preach terrorism or those professing these religions are terrorists? Certainly not. The blood of thousands at the doors of churches, mosques, temples, synagogues, etc., cannot permit us to draw an inference that the religions of which they are the symbols preach violence or blood-shed. Every religion is the religion of peace. In such matters, objective approach should be adopted. All world leaders including Indian Prime Ministers as also other international personalities have condemned terrorism clearly stating that all religions should be respected because there is no room for terrorism or violence in any religion or any civilised world of which we are a part. All of us must take statements of all such persons in the right earnest.

Islam, like all other primal religions of the world, does not permit or sanction use of force against innocent people. Islam is the religion of peace, tranquility and non-violence. **Islam is not one what a functional Muslim does; Islam is one what a true Muslim should do.** Islam is a non-sectarian, non-racial, non-doctrinal religion. It expects Muslims to do what is right and permissible and refrain from doing what is forbidden. A true Muslim must ensure that justice prevails and injustice is defeated. Thus, Islam is a religion that lives not for itself but for the whole of humankind. The following extract from *Surah-Al-Imran* (S.3) bears testimony to it:

> "Ye are the best of Peoples, evolved for humankind.
>
> Enjoining what is right, Forbidding what is wrong."

(*Thus anyone teaching or preaching anything contrary to that cannot be a true Muslim and cannot claim to be one of the best of peoples evolved for humankind*).

In Islam life of human being or any other creature is considered to be the most precious and valuable possession of the living being. Islam advocates security of life and personal liberty of every human being and compassionate treatment even to animals. No Muslim is permitted to take law in his own hands and kill any innocent person or even a person who has committed any offence or sin. In *Surah-Al-Maida* (5A-32), it is so ordained and the relevant portion of the *Surah* is quoted below:

That if any one slew,

A person-unless it be,

For murder or for speaking,

Mischief in the land,

It would be as if,

He slew the whole people.

It is clearly evident from the above quotation that killing of an innocent person is as if the killer has murdered the whole of humanity or, in other words, the entire community. On the other hand, if anyone saves an innocent person, he or she renders service to the entire community and in that way saves the whole country. Thus, condemnation of individual assassination and revenge is the very essence of Islamic tenets. According to the Quran, the whole of humankind is a single nation as so ordained in *surah* 49:13:

"O mankind! We created,

You from a single (pair),

Of a male and female,

And made you into,

Nations and tribes, that

Ye may know each other".

Quran further ordains:

"And among His Signs,

Is this, that He created,

For you mates from among,
Yourselves, that ye may,
Dwell in tranquility with them,
And He was put love,
And mercy between you (hearts):
Verily in that are Signs,
For those who reflect." (S-30: 21),
And among His Signs,
Is the creation of the heavens,
And the earth, and the variations,
In your languages,
And your colours: verily,
In that are Signs,
For those who know. (S-30: 22)

The variations in languages and colours may be viewed from the geographical aspect or from the aspect of periods of time. All mankind were created of a single pair of parents; yet they have spread to different countries and climates and developed different languages and different shades of complexions. And yet their basic unity remains unaltered. They feel in the same way, and are all equally under Allah's care. Then there are the variations in time. Old languages die out, new ones are evolved. New conditions of life and thought are constantly evolving new words and expressions, new syntactical structures, and new modes of pronunciation. Even old races die, and new races are born.

According to *Surah-Al-Baqraah* (S.2A), as stated above, mankind was a single nation. To quote:

Mankind was one single nation,

And Allah sent Messengers,

with glad tidings and warnings,

And with them He sent,

The Book in truth,

To Judge between people,

In matters wherein,

They differed.

In *Surah An-Nisa*, the mankind includes not only Muslims but all human beings, irrespective of the religion they profess, the language they speak, the country they live in and the race they belong to. To quote:

O Mankind! Fear

You're Guardian Lord,

Who created you

From a single Person.

Surah Yunus also carries the same message. To quote:

"mankind was but one nation,

But differed (later)."

Thus, whole of humankind was created one, and Allah's Message to humankind is in essence one, the Message of Unity and Truth. But as selfishness and egotism got hold of man, certain differences sprang up between individuals, races, and nations, and in His infinite Mercy He sent them messages and messages to suit their varying mentality, to test them by His gifts, and stir them up to emulation in virtue and piety.

In Islam, there is no question of race, caste, colour, creed, etc. *Surah Al-Ambia* also carries a similar message. To quote:

"We sent thee not, but

As a Mercy for all creatures."

The positive and objective interpretation of this part of the *surah* clearly reveals that there is no question now of race or nation, of a "chosen people" or the "seed of Abraham", or the "seed of David"; or of Hindu Arya-varta; of Jew or Gentile, Arab or 'Ajam (non-Arab), Turk or Tajik, European or Asiatic, white or coloured; Aryan, Semitic, Mongolian, or African; or American, Australian, or Polynesian. To all men and creatures other than men who have any spiritual responsibility, the principles universally apply.

It is evident from the details, recorded above, that any sins or follies committed by the followers of any religion cannot be attributed to their respective religions. They (the terrorists or persons involved in violence) are to be condemned and not the religion they profess.

A human being may become emotional, aggressive or violent in an emotionally charged situation, but there is a spiritual urge in every person for peace. Even if a person is violent now, he or she may cease to be so with the passage of time. If some of the persons who were involved in communal holocaust during the partition of India, and are alive, are asked to repeat the same things today, they, undoubtedly, will show the white flag because every human being, being inwardly instinctive, intellectual and super conscious, yearns for peace and one can notice qualities of unity and oneness, humility, peace, compassion, love, helpfulness, etc., reflected in his or her personal behaviour and outlook sooner or later. Violence is a reflection of fear, anger, greed, jealousy and hatred and sometimes a symbol of retaliation which creates rift between individuals, groups of people, communities, followers of different religions and nations though the UN Charter refers to all of us as "the peoples of the world." The preamble of the UN Charter reads as under:

Preamble of the United Nations Character

to save succeeding generations from the scourge of war, which twice in our life-time has brought untold sorrow to mankind, and

to reaffirm faith in fundamental human rights, in the dignity and worth of the human person, in the equal rights of men and women and of nations large and small, and

to establish conditions under which justice and respect for the obligations arising from treaties and other sources of international law can be maintained, and

to promote social progress and better standards of life in larger freedom.

to practice tolerance and live together in peace with one another as good neighbours, and

to unite our strength to maintain international peace and security, and to employ international machinery for the promotion of the economic and social advancement of all peoples.

Hence, there is no justification for hating or condemning any religion, community, country or nation how muchsoever compelling the situation may be.

Reference

1. League of Nations Council Debate on International Terrorism, November-December 1934. Speech of M. Laval quoted in R.A. Friedlander, *Terrorism-Documents of International and Local Control*, referred to as Friedlander, Vol. 1, (1979), p. 217.

5

Right to Hate in the Context of Hindu-Muslim Relationship

Hate

We are told that we should hate the 'sin' and not the sinner, but the things are changing rapidly and the real ground situation has a different story to tell. We have started not only to hate the sinner as also the religion and the followers of the religion he or she professes as also the country to which he or she belongs, though there is no cogent reason for doing so. How 'A' is accountable for the acts of omission and commission done/not done by 'B' even if B may be his/her sibling, follower of the religion B professes, or the national of the country of his/her origin. We, however, have a right to criticise or take legal action against the erring persons whosoever and wherever they may be.

There are bad elements in every society and they, instead of creating amity among various sections of the society, prefer to disrupt the unity and have scant regard for their societal obligations. Sometimes, a critic may be genuine one and sincere but, at the same time, he must read the pulse of the society, be it local, national or international, because the whole of humankind is a single nation and we should know that if we do anything that hurts the feelings of any class of people or followers of any particular religion it will be a disservice to the whole of humanity, particularly when we know that followers of almost all the religions are, by and large, religiously sensitive. Degree of sensitivity may vary from one to the other depending on one's background, culture, values, beliefs and convictions. Even then we find that persons belonging to all major religions of the world have been indicted for criticising other religions and beliefs orally and through their writings.

Liberty of expression, which is a basic human right, does not permit us to say or write that hurts the feelings of any class of people because the word "people" is a pluralistic term and its integrity should not be disintegrated. Even otherwise, there is a common saying that there are certain norms even in madness.

Thus, we have no right to hate anyone, but we have a right to criticise or express our views, as mentioned above, within permissible parameters. We have no moral right to embrace or indulge in any evil idea, tendency or practice or writings or commentaries just to create ill-will amongst people for so-called fame, name and popularity. Sometimes, even literature based on truth may be harmful from the humanitarian point of view. Morality and religious instructions may not have any legal support, but their societal value and sanctity cannot be ignored. Morality and law are also inter-linked and inter-woven otherwise sexual crimes would not have been treated as crimes and would have been treated as mere biological requirement and all prohibitory laws, mostly based on morality, would not have been framed.

Hate Speeches

Likewise, no one has a right to make any hate speeches as it is not only the violation of municipal laws but it is gross violation of international norms and negation of the UN General Assembly resolutions adopted in December 1994 session- one dealing with "contemporary forms of racism, racial discrimination, xenophobia and related intolerance," and the other, related to "the acts of violence, of intolerance and of discrimination on the grounds of religion and belief, and condemning" "all instances of hatred, intolerance and acts of violence, intimidation and coercion motivated by religious extremism and intolerance." Even inflammatory political speeches and religious sermons have no place in a civilised society. Freedom of speech is of paramount value in a liberal democratic society, but unfettered liberty is no liberty and no one is at liberty to violate the law or to hurt anyone emotionally, physically or through gestures. Even the proposed bill regarding prevention of communal violence titled **'Prevention of Communal and Targeted Violence (Access to Justice and Reparations) BILL, 2011'** also contains a provision (section 8) to ban hate propaganda. To quote:

Hate propaganda: Notwithstanding anything contained in any other law for the time being in force, whoever publishes, communicates or disseminates by words, either spoken or written, or by signs or by visible representation or by electronic or other means of mass communication or otherwise acts inciting hatred causing clear danger of violence against a group or persons belonging to that group, in general or specifically, or disseminates or broadcasts any information, or publishes or displays any advertisement or notice, that could reasonably be construed to demonstrate an intention to promote or incite hatred or expose or is likely to expose the group or persons belonging to that group to such hatred, is said to be guilty of hate propaganda.

Provided that nothing will be deemed to be hate propaganda, which is done in furtherance of or promotes fundamental rights enshrined in Chapter III of the Constitution of India.

Section 112 deals with the Punishment for hate propaganda and provides that the offence of hate propaganda shall be punishable with imprisonment which may extend to three years or fine or both.

Those still adhering to the following views, be in absolute minority, are out and out to sabotage the cause of Hindu-Muslim unity. **They should learn to accept what they cannot change.**

The So-called Hindu View

Hindu-Muslim unity is a mirage for some of them. They go on repeating that Muslims are the invaders, they looted the country, forced Hindus to embrace Islam, destroyed the temples, broke the idols, raped the women and heaped innumerable indignities on the people of this country. They are also of the view that what could not be achieved during the last thousand years cannot be achieved in ensuing thousand years. They should change their mind-set failing which the concept of *sarva dharma sambhava* or secularism of which they feel proud shall have no meaning.

Such persons should go through the following quotations from Quran and other Islamic literature. No pick and choose please. They should not get confused with the words like *Kafir*, *Allah* etc., *Allah* is an Arabic word which means God in English, *Ishwar* in Hindi and *Khuda* in Persian and other equivalents in more than 2000 languages of the world, say, Dios in Spanish, Theo's in Greek, Dio in Italian, Deus in Portuguese, Gott in German, Dumnezeu in Romanian, Dieu in French, to name a few. Does it mean that we have separate Gods. God is one and one only. Other may be gods and *devtas.* They also command respect and reverence from their followers but, at the same time, those who do not believe in such gods and *devtas* they are also required to have full regard for their religious sanctity to their followers. Thus, our Hindu brothers must realise that Hindus and Muslims have to live in this country as one people, the people of India.

The So-called Muslim View Quotes from Scriptures

It is alleged that brotherhood of Islam is not the universal brotherhood of men. It is brotherhood of Muslims for Muslims only. For those who are outside is nothing but contempt and enmity. Such views are contrary to what is ordained or mentioned in religious scriptures and holy books of Hindus and Muslims. Only God or detailed study of religious literature with open eyes and a larger heart can help them in understanding the things in proper perspective, otherwise the concepts like *vasudev kutumbakam* (the whole world is a family), world being a global village, universality of human rights, globalisation, etc., will have no meaning for them and their subjective approach may take them nowhere. They may laugh at persons like us today but tomorrow is ours.

The Hindus and Muslims should avoid CONTROVERSIAL QUESTIONS ABOUT EACH OTHER'S RELIGION AND HISTORY because answers to these questions will lead to various counter-questions and it may prove to be an endless exercise. I came across such questions during my day-to-day life in India as also during surfing the net and found that both Hindu and Muslim youth and those with subjective and biased approach are still living in an illusory world and have not reconciled to the changed global scenario. These misguided Hindus and Muslims who are bent upon perpetuating the feelings of enmity, malice and hatred against each other must read the following quotations from religious scriptures of both the religions. Most of these quotations are self-explanatory and are a clear indication that no religion speaks of negation of human values and it is also the indicative index for those who are out and out to lay their hands only on such portions of these scriptures that may have dual interpretations or may create ill-will amongst the followers of different religions and their only agenda is to disturb peace and strike at all channels of peace and tranquility. For them, Hindu-Muslim unity is bull-shit.

Quotes from *Bhagavad Gita* and the *Vedas*, etc.

Bhagvad Geeta

Fear Not. What is not real never was and never will be. What is real always was and cannot be destroyed.

One must learn to endure fleeting things

They come and go

Neither in this world nor elsewhere is there any happiness in store for him who always doubts.

An ignorant man is lost, faithless, and filled with self-doubt;

A soul that harbours doubt has no joy, not in this world or the next.

the security of any other state, even its observance would be on no higher a moral plane than the honesty that is popularly supposed to exist among thieves. India having accepted Aśoka's great ideal of *dharmavijaya* or conquest by Righteousness, it was inevitable that this very Buddhist *maitrī*, or love and goodwill towards all, should form the ultimate spiritual basis of her policy of dynamic neutrality in world affairs. It is the *raison d'etre* of the fact that, while working unremittingly for world peace, the Government of India consistently refuses to align itself with any power bloc. Such an attitude has naturally drawn her closer to the Buddhist countries of South-East Asia, whose respective policies are naturally inspired by one and the same ideal. But by its very nature, such a relationship does not and cannot imply hostility or even indifference towards any other. country or group of countries. In fact, it is not one political group among other groups, with its own exclusive preferences and limited loyalties, but rather a slowly expanding centre radiating to the world the impersonal, universal and neutral power of *maitrī.* It is in this light that one must view the Government of India's attempts to renew her ancient ties with the countries of Asia. It is because Buddhism alone can provide the necessary basis for these attempts that its political implications for Asia, and through Asia for the whole world, are so enormous and so important.

Buddhism has remained a cultural force in Europe, and Russell has gone so far as to declare that if he were compelled to choose between the religions of the world he would choose Buddhism. We may recall that Schopenhauer, in the second decade of the nineteenth century, had declared himself a Buddhist, and following him Nietzsche, and still later Wittgenstein have become intellectual forces looking back to Buddhism, and motivating what now goes under the banner of postmodernism.

But more importantly, let us not forget that the Buddha aimed at the development of a new type of freemen, free from prejudices, intent on working out his own future, with reliancç on one' own self, *ātmadīpa*. As Radhakrishnan has pointed out that the Buddha is an outstanding representative of our religious tradition, and his teachings have become integral part of our culture. In a sense, says Radhakrishnan, the Buddha is a maker of modern Hinduism (*2500 Years of Buddhism*, p. xvi, The Publications Division, New Delhi, 1959).

The Buddha's humanism had crossed racial and national barriers. Yet the chaotic condition of world affairs reflects the chaos in man's souls. History has become universal in spirit. Its subject matter is neither Europe nor Asia, neither East nor West, but humanity in all lands and ages. In spite of political divisions, the world is one, whether we like it or not. The fortunes of everyone are linked up with those of others. But we are suffering from an exhaustion of spirit, an increase of egoism, individual and collective, which seem to make the ideal of a world society too difficult to desire. What we need today is a spiritual view of the universe. We must recover the lost ideal of spiritual freedom *ātmalābhan na param vidyate.* If we wish to achieve peace we must maintain that inner harmony, that poise of soul, which are the essential elements of peace. We must possess ourselves even though all else is lost. The free spirit sets no bounds to its love, recognises in all human beings a spark of holiness, and offers itself up as a willing victim to the cause of mankind. It casts off all fear except that of wrong doing, passes the bounds of time and death and finds inexhaustible power in life eternal. Let us not forget that Buddhism is a religion of kindness, humanity and equality.

8

The Resurgence of the Bodhisattva Ideal

I

The Resurgence of the Bodhisattva Ideal in Recent Indian Thought

The term 'recent' spans centuries, and overlaps with 'modern' in the sense that Descartes is held as a modern philosopher. In Indian context, 'recent' and 'modern' maps the new age that dawned in the nineteenth century, in the wake of British system of education and revaluation of the medieval values and ways of life. There has been the problem with Buddhism in so far as our cultural attitude and beliefs concerning the Buddha's teachings of the Way. Historically the disappearance of Buddhism from the Indian scene has been a problem issue with the general trend of Hindu ideal of life and practice. Hindu mind has always been uncomfortable with the Buddhist thesis of *anātmavāda*, and *kṣanabhangavāda*. These two have been the points of attack by non-Buddhist schools. Udayana wrote the *Ātmatattvaviveka* with the sole intention of refuting the Buddhist thesis of *anātma* or *niḥsvabhāvatā*. Kumārila's tirade against Buddhism took the form of a frontal attack in the *Bauddhadhikkāra*. But Kumārila had respect for Buddhist ethics. He had the honesty to admit that the Buddhist code of conduct emphasing *ahimsā* is a noble one, though its repudiation of the Vedas is ignoble. For Kumārila, the truth of Buddhism is mixed up with much that is false, and so he compares it to the milk put in the dog's skin, *Śvācarmanikṣipta kṣiravad* (*Tantravārttika*, 1.3.6). Usually Śaṁkara is credited with routing Buddhism out of India. But this is a stupid and ignorant notion. In the *Brahmasūtra bhāṣya*, Śaṁkara had argued against a good many philosophical schools like Vaiśeṣika, Sāṁkhya, Jainism, the Pāśupat and Pañcaratra views, besides a couple of shades of Buddhism, comprising the Vaibhāṣika, Sautāntrika and Vijñānavāda. The Buddhist schools apart, the schools and the views rebutted by Śaṁkara have been thriving as before. But why should the disappearance of Buddhism is ascribed to Śaṁkara's critique of it? Philosophical wrangling can never the cause of the disappearance of any school. There must have been historical reasons of which Hindu culture and philosophy remains gleefully ignorant and indifferent to. Many would say that Kumārila critiqued Buddhism, but no one mentions that Śāntarakṣita gave a fitting reply to Kumārila in *Tattvasaṁgraha*. The older school of the Nyāya had Buddhism as its chief philosophical opponent or *pūrva pakṣa*, while the later development of Nyāya had the Mimāṁsaka as the major contender. This change is significant historically. In our times, Daya Krishna has raised the question urging philosophers to look into the causes of the change of philosophical climate. The Brāhminical line of thinking felt unformatable with the Buddhist mode of metaphysical thinking. To some it appeared that the Buddhists lacked philosophical or metaphysical depth. Vivekananda, for example, remarked that the Buddhist thought was lacking in metaphysics. He said, "I do not endorse all his philosophy. I want a good deal of metaphysics for myself" (*Selections* from Vivekananda, p. 361, Advaita Ashram, Kolkata, 2007). It appears that Vivekananda had Pali Buddhism in mind when he made the remark, for Sanskrit Buddhism, or Mahāyāna in particular, is quite sophisticated an affair in the matter of metaphysical depth and probing. A perusal of his writings reveals to us that Vivekananda had never encountered Nāgārjuna's or Candrakirṭi's dialectical writings. In one of his lectures Vivekananda touches the Vijñānavāda thesis of momentariness of consciousness, but that closely follows Śaṁkara's footsteps, in taking side with the Advaita response to the Buddhist point of view. But there can be no doubt about the fact that Vivekananda had unbounded regard and respect for the Buddha, and he had been a great admirer of the ethical excellence that the Buddha embodied. For Vivekananda, the Buddha stood for the great ethical ideal, absolutely disinterested altruism, and he appropriated the Buddha's classic call to work for the good and happiness of the many in his own missionary agenda.

There has been ambivalence on the part of our cultural leaders, and this consists in separating the person of the Buddha from his teachings. His teachings had made the sensibility of the followers of the Brāhminical lineage of culture and life somewhat uncomfortable. So the Buddha's moral personality is held in high esteem, while casting his teachings away. There is a notable feature amongst our modern thinkers. What could be the reason for the ambivalence?

Radhakrishnan touched upon this issue with the remark that it is not true that Buddhism have left no trace in the lineage of Indian philosophical thinking. The alleged disappearance is to be understood as having gone sub-terrainian. The best and noble elements of the Buddhist heritage have been absorbed into the Hindu way of life and culture. Of our recent thinkers, Radhakrishnan alone paid a greater attention to the Buddhist thought in his writings. He translated the *Dhammapada* with a commentary, lectured on the Buddha in the Master Mind series to the British Academy, and above all, the masterful discussion on Vijñānavāda and Nāgārjuna in the first volume of *Indian Philosophy*.

The point is that there has been a conscious endeavour at accommodating the Buddha and his teachings as a valued integral part of the Indian heritage. Tilak, for instance, devoted a section on the Buddha and the Pali Buddhist philosophical writings in his celebrated commentary on the *Gītā*. The trend continued through such other important thinkers like Rabindranath Tagore and Sri Aurobindo.

Let us take the case of Rabindranath Tagore. He was born in a family that espoused the beliefs of reformed Hindu Church, the Brāhmo Samaj, founded by Rammohan Ray. Rabindranath's father, Debendranath was the leader of the church, and compiled its scripture, the *Brāhmadharma*. It has selections of non-idolatrous, and non-advaitic passages from the Upaniṣad, and no less importantly from the *Dhammapada*, besides such works as the *Mahābhārata* and the *Mahānirvāṇa Tantra*, etc. Rabindranath, all through his life put *Upaniṣad* on the same pedestal in the company of the *Dhammapada*. He looked upon the both as forming one unbroken spiritual inheritance through history. This was a matter of the spirit, and for Rabindranath there was no Brāhminical-Buddhist divide.

Rabindranath was drawn towards such Buddhist values as *maitrī* and the ideal of *Brahmavihāra*. He wrote an essay in explication of the metaphor of the mother in the *Metta Sūtta* of the *Sūtta Nipāta.* It was for him the great moral ideal to be inculcated in society. He was one of the pioneers of Buddhist studies and invited scholars to translate and write on the Buddhist moral ideas at the centre he founded in Santineketan. He travelled to Buddhist countries and noticed how Buddhism helped the flourishing of art and culture wherever it was taken to. As for his contribution to the spread of Buddhism in the domain of culture he wrote poems and dramas on Buddhist themes, and these stand to attest both his creative genius as a literary artist as well as his unfailing admiration for the Buddha and his compassionate teachings.

Vivekananda regarded the Buddha as the highest point of man's spiritual evolution. He called it "the Buddha-man", "the greatest man that was ever born" (*Selections from Vivekananda*, p. 53, and other entries under Buddha and Buddhism). Vivekananda took the Buddha standing as "the perfection of the active type" (*ibid.* p. 362) and he wished if he "had one infinitesimal part of Buddha's heart". He even went to the extent of saying that Buddha was his *ishta*. On this point a portion of his letter (dated February, 1890) is worth quoting: "Lord Budddha is my Ishta-my God. He preached no theory about Godhead-he was himself God, I fully believe it". (*Letter*-12, p.19, Adwaita Ashram, Kolkata, 2008). This is a remarkable statement hardly ever taken note of. Yet apart from his personal adoration of the Buddha, Vivekananda considered the social element of Buddhism to be the most unique. The Buddha's deep all-embracing humanism was at the root of his practice of *brahma-vihāra*. Vivekananda referred to it as "the Buddha's heart": "that sympathy, that love, that heart, that thinks for all, until Buddha's heart comes once more into India...., there is no hope for us" (*Selections*, p. 273). And as for the relationship of Buddhism to Hinduism, Vivekananda had no qualms about the fact that the Buddha was "the fulfilment, the logical conclusion, the logical development of the religion of the Hindus", and again, "The separation between the Buddhists and the Brahmins is the cause of the downfall of India" (*ibid,* pp. 16-17).

This Buddhology, as envisaged and formulated so passionately by Vivekananda reappears in Sri Aurobindo's evolutionary philosophy. In *The Life Divine*, Sri Aurobindo distinguishes between the two poises of Brahman, silent and active. Silence and Activity flow into each other, and Sri Aurobindo takes the case of the Buddha as exemplifying the modalities of the Real, and says, "Thus was it possible for the Buddha to attain the state of *Nirvaṇa* and yet act puissantly in the world, impersonal in his inner consciousness, in his action the most powerful personality that we know of as having lived and produced results upon earth" (*The Life Divine*, New York, 1949, pp. 29-30). Again, later in that work Sri Aurobindo formulates his ideal of the gnostic being. The concept of 'gnostic being' tolls back to the Mahāyana ideal of Bodhisattva. In the life of the gnostic being, there is "a close and complete consciousness of the self of others, a consciousness of their mind, life, physical being which are felt as if they were one's own. The gnostic being will act, not out of a surface sentiment of love and sympathy or any similar feeling, but out of this close mutual consciousness, this intimate oneness" (*ibid.* p. 913). Anyone familiar with Śāntideva's *Bodhicaryāvatāra* would at once recall the twin processes of *parātma samatā* and *parātma parivartana* requisite for the bodhisattva to act for the good of others. The moral agent has to realise his oneness (*samatā*) with others who are in suffering and need help. In the process the bodhisattva transforms (*parivartana*) his self into the self of others. The point is that unqualified spontaneous altruism becomes possible only the twin metaphysical processes. (See *Bodhicaryāvatāra*, Chapter VIII, Verse 137-139).

There can be no doubt as regards the foundational experience for motivelessness of altruism to be possible at all looks back the Buddhist formulation as indicated above. In some form or other, all the leaders of recent Indian thought have spelled their views and theories around the basic Buddhist insight. Sri Aurobindo has been the first ever to point to this chain of the ideal. The spiritually realised, the liberated man is preoccupied with the good of all beings; Buddha discovering the way of *Nirvāṇa* must turn back to open that way to those who are still under the delusion of their constructive instead of their real being—or non-being; Vivekananda, drawn by the Absolute, feels also the call of the disguised Godhead in humanity and most the call of the fallen and the suffering, the call of the self to the self in the obscure body of the universe" (*ibid,* pp. 930-31). How are we explain or understand the linkage: the Buddha, Vivekananda and Sri Aurobindo's conception of the gnostic being. There can be no doubt that it is in point of fact a resurgence of the bodhisattva ideal in our own times.

Let us connect three assertions to this effect. There is first one quote from Rabindranath Tagore: "If the world passes on in tears how could I sit alone pursuing my own salvation?" Vivekananda wrote to his brother monks: "Of what consequence is it to the world if I on or I attain mukti? We have to take the whole world to mukti". The Dalai Lama, who is avowedly a follower of the *Bodhisattva yāna*, has told to Claude B. Levenson: "I, for the greater good of living being, I had to be reincarnated as, say a bridge or an insect, as a monk who follows the Mahāyāna it is my duty to do it. As long as there are beings who suffer, I shall return". (*The Dalai Lama*, p. 272, Oxford University Press, 2006). The bodhisattva lives and dies for others. The ideal has stood out through centuries as a paradigm of moral perfection. The jīvanmukta may live for others, but does not die for them. Altruism is the *raison d'etre* of a bodhisattva's existence. In India, it was Appayya Dikṣita who adumbrated the ideal of *sarvamukti*, as the logical goal of Vedāntic ethical development. For him, *sarvamukti* was theological necessity, an implication for *eka-jīva-vāda*, the doctrine of the unity of all *jīvas*. It suggests that there is only one *jīva*. However, Appayya Dikṣita did not get a hearing from the orthodox Vedāntins. For them, *mukti* was a solitary ritual. On the other hand, the details of the bodhisattva ideal had changed, interpretations had differed, certain ideas had evolved, others lost in importance, refinements were made in the stages of the path. It was a dynamic, living ideal. And at the hands of recent Indian thinkers, the ideal has been adapted to modern needs. The heart of the ideal, its essence, has remained the same. It has received a new life, new expression and new authority through writings of the thinkers we have mentioned above. We may add further that Gandhi's concept of *sarvodaya* obviously bears the streaks of bodhisattva inspiration. His idea of Truth, as the unity of all living beings, implies the ethics of non-violence.

II

Engaged Buddhism: Social and Political Visions of Ambedkar's Neo-Buddhism

We shall now turn to a more recent phenomenon of Buddhist socio-political movement as led by Ambedkar, for which the grounds were prepared by the thinkers and their ideas in theoretical form.

Like all religions Buddhism has experienced reform movements throughout history to restore the original core values of the faith when leadership and institutions have fallen into decay. Korea, Japan, Thailand and Sri Lanka, Myanmar, and India have not been exceptions to the general statement. Modern Buddhism in Asia is not just a meditative vehicle for spiritual liberation, but is now also a vehicle that includes liberation movements for social and political change. What has come to be known as "socially engaged Buddhism" or simply "engaged Buddhism" is a vast array of Asian movements, dedicated to addressing the economic, social, political and environmental as well as the spiritual needs of modern humankind. For example, in South-East Asia Buddhist monks work with lay volunteers to rejuvenate village life. In South Asia Indian untouchables have converted to form a Buddhist movement for social change and put an end to the misery of caste system. In East Asia Buddhist lay movements have drawn millions of members by caring for their daily needs. And throughout Asia, Buddhist nuns are founding orders that work for institutional changes in the Buddhist monastic communities and organise social, educational, and health services for the poor. And, their response to this situation is not only to help people practice spirituality for the sake of personal liberation, but also to change the economic system for the sake of social liberation. The Buddhist ideal encouraged positive activities. Ambedkar's admonition is there on record. He urged his disciples to go out and serve the people in the amelioration of their lot. The phrase of his admonition is famously well-known: *vahujana hitāya, vahujana sukhāya*. The great Buddhist king Aśoka in the Buddhist history (268-233 BCE) represents a model Buddhist ruler who always had his subject's economic and social well-being as his main concerns, and the great Indian philosopher Nāgārjuna advised a king (see *Ratnāvali*, 231-321) to govern with a compassionate socialism that included education for the people, fixed charges for doctors, socially supported healthcare, and low taxes. Engaged Buddhism has its meaning in the reconstructive prospects, based on the Buddha's method of deconstruction, for all sentient beings.

In Asia people look forward to reconstructing their identity as Buddhists with the correct Buddhism socially.

Ambedkar came to Buddhism through his critique of Hinduism formulated in terms of the social stratification based on caste systems. His general stand was that a people and their religion must be judged by social standards based on social ethics. He was of the opinion that religions are for the society and not society for religion. But what were Ambedkar's reasons for choosing Buddhism? In *The Buddha and His Dhamma* he has highlighted the features of Buddhism as follows:

1. Buddhism emphasised the role of reason as against faith or superstition.

2. Buddhism rejected many objects of dogmatic belief such as God and soul (Book IV, Part I).

3. Buddhism was opposed to caste system (Book III, Part V, Section 4).

4. Buddhism emphasised morality as an essence of good life. Morality in Buddhism is essentially human-centric and had no reference to soul and God (Book IV, Part I, Section 5).

Thus it was the rational, secular, moral and egalitarian aspects of Buddhism.

Ambedkar argued for reinterpreting Buddhism, since in spite of there being many progressive elements, egalitarian, secular and rational, these are not stated consistently and coherently, but are mixed with many regressive elements, such as rebirth and re-death, higher and lower worlds, etc. Buddhism comes down to us with myths and superstitions. The idea of suffering as a noble truth did not appeal to Ambedkar. According to him the element of pessimism is an undesirable element. He thought that Buddhism has a social message. The monks were urged by the Buddha to strive for the well-being and happiness of the many. He was disappointed to observe how the monks cared more for their personal liberation. Ambedkar wanted the monks to play a social role as missionaries and social workers. And lastly, he disapproved the division of Buddhism into various sects like Theravāda and Mahāyāna. He was inclined towards Theravāda for its realist ontology and morality in its approach to values. He sought to combine the best elements of Theravāda and Mahāyāna. He appreciated the Mahāyāna doctrine of *pāramitās* with emphasis on *prajñā* and *karuṇā* in his interpretation and reconstruction of Buddhism.

Ambedkara offered an alternative explanation of the Buddha's renunciation. He was influenced by Dharmananda Kosambi's researches in Pali Buddhism. The historical background of Siddarth's developing detachment and disinclination towards worldly life is the conflicts between Sākya and Koliya clans on the issue of sharing the water of the river Rohini. Seeing that people constantly fighting with each other, Gotama developed detachment and disinclination towards the life in the world. Further Ambedkar tries to show that the so called suffering pervading the whole of human life was in fact the suffering which arises out of one's social existence involving conflicts, inequality and injustices that bothered Gotama. In the light of Ambedkara's interpretation one can say that though Gotama's disenchantment with the worldly life was occasioned by Sākhya-Koliya war, he generalised this phenomenon of war into the general problem of conflict including in it even class struggle and caste struggle.

The important aspect of Ambedkar's interpretations of the Buddha's life is its demythologised characters. Adale Ficke and Christoph Emmridh have shown in their researches that Ambedkar sought to interpret was Buddhist scriptures to project the Buddha as a social reformer. (See S. Jondhale and Johames Beltz, *Reconstructing the World: B.R. Ambedkar and Buddhism in India*, Oxford University Press, New Delhi, 2004).

As for the pessimism of the teaching of the four Noble Truths, Ambedkar seeks to give an optimistic interpretation of the doctrine of suffering. He rejects the traditional interpretation, and suggests a realistic and empirical linc of approach in lieu of the usual transcendental-metaphysical approach. So he restated the doctrine leaving room for hope and optimism, to show that a happy life in this world is indeed possible. Instead of saying that the world is of the nature of suffering, Ambedkar says that there is suffering in the world. Now the problem of suffering becomes the problem of removing the suffering from the world and not that of running away from the world itself. As he says, the world is full of suffering, but how to remove the suffering from the world is the only purpose of Dhamma.

There is more to Ambedkar's reconstruction of the traditional view of the doctrine of suffering, but these need not detain us. On the contrary, we propose to concentrate on the following elements of his reconstruction:

(a) The path of purity. He calls them the five "principles of life", the five-fold *śīla.*

(b) Under the title "The Doctrine of Virtue", Ambedkar includes the Mahāyāna doctrine of the *pāramitās,* or the states of perfection in virtues with emphasis on *prajñā-pāramitā*. There is a great emphasis on morality in Ambedkar's understanding of Buddhism. And morality, in traditional Buddhism is represented by *śīla*. This could be the reason why he thought that *śīla* was central theme in the Buddha's first sermon.

In the Mahāyāna lineage it is held that not one, but three *dharmacakra* sermons were delivered by the Buddha. The first sermon enunciates the doctrine of suffering, the second formulates the doctrine of *pāramitās*, and the third and the final one develop the doctrine of *vijñānavāda*. Ambedkar clubs the first and the second sermons together and holds that the doctrine of *pāramitās* was the theme the first sermon itself.

Dhamma is the second of the three jewels of Buddhism. Ambedkar's conception is an important part of his reconstruction of Buddhism. In simple terms, he identifies *dhamma* with morality and tries to remove various misconceptions. In Sanskrit, the word dharma is a polyguous term, and is popularly taken to mean religion. Does the Pali word *dhamma* share the same characteristic? Ambedkar denies the possibility in absolute terms. He tries to eliminate the traditional doctrines of karma and rebirth and presents a secular this worldly formulation of Buddhism. He is averse to associating Buddhism with any kind of transcendence or other worldliness.

Ambedkar contradistinguishes the Buddha's *dhamma* from other religions. In most religious belief in transcendental entities like God, soul and other worlds become the basis of morality. There operates the idea of morality as divine commandment. In interpreting Buddhism, Ambedkar makes morality the root of religion. Morality is the essence of the *dhamma*. Ambedkar reconstructs Buddhism in such a manner as by placing morality at the centre, while religious beliefs are made to rotate around it. The notions of karma and rebirth are mutually linked up and suggest a trans-empirical import. Ambedkar delinked the issues and restated then differently. He found the two doctrines inconsistent with the Buddhist view of *anātmavāda*, i.e., the denial of a continuous or constant identity of the moral agent. He denied the karma doctrine as it was traditionally understood and reinterpreted it in such a way that it no more implies the usual notion of rebirth. Ambedkar denied rebirth if it meant rebirth of a soul or rebirth of the same person. He understands death and rebirth in physical terms, he made the doctrine of rebirth independent of the doctrine of karma and rendered it morally neutral.

We may now turn to considering Ambedkar's justification of *dhamma*.

If *dhamma* is morality, and if this morality is not justified either on God's command, or on the basis of the doctrine of karma, or rebirth, then what is the *dhamma*-morality itself? Now Ambedkar is not a deontologist like Kant, so we may not say that for him morality is intrinsically justified. It appears that Ambedkar is a sort of consequentialist. The upholders of karma doctrine were also consequentialists. They hold that moral actions are to be performed keeping in mind their consequences to be borne by the agent. Ambedkar holds that morally good actions are to be performed for their consequences on the humanity at large. "Do *kuśala karma* so that humanity may benefit by a good moral order which a *kuśala karma* helps to sustain, do not do *akuśala karma* for humanity will suffer from bad moral order which an *akuśala karma* will bring about" (*The Buddha and His Dhamma*, III. VI. 25). This view may be called universal consequentialism. This morality is not transcendental. *Dhamma*, for Ambedkar's interpretation is a secular way of life based on morality, which aims at well-being of the whole humanity. Hence *dhamma* being secular morality is distinguished from the way of life based on belief in any supernatural power like God or ritual potency, nor is it rooted in speculative metaphysics or blind faith in some scriptures. One may develop freedom from passions and craving by realising the impermanence of all things and attain moral perfection.

Ambedkar identifies the category of *saddhamma* with the Buddha's teaching, and it forms an important part of his reconstruction of Buddhism. *Saddhamma* is alternatively called philosophy of Dhamma. It may be noted that Ambedkar uses the term 'philosophy' for a total social perspective, or we may call it his sociology of religion.

Dhamma refers initially to an individually moral perspective. Then the individual perspective becomes a social phenomenon by taking on dimension of moral relationships among all the members of the society. This is what Ambedkar calls *saddhamma.*

According to Ambedkar the social moral perspective of Buddhism consists of the principles like *prajñā, maitrī* and *karuṇā. Prajñā* in traditional Buddhism refers to wisdom concerning impermanence of whatever that exists, and the *anattā* doctrine. But Ambedkar gives it a more general form to include knowledge in general and learning which is to be made available to all. Ambedkar holds that over and above *prajñā*, *karuṇā* and *maitrī* are equally important as the part of *saddhamma*. He made the social reformation by way of eradicating caste-*varṇa* barriers and advocating equality an important part of *saddhamma*. *Dhamma* becomes *saddhamma* when individual moral pursuits of the people contribute to the general social good, which, in turn, leads to the establishment of an ideal society based on perfect justice. For Ambedkar the religion of the Buddha is perfect justice springing from a man's own meritorious disposition.

Ambedkar's notion of ideal society deserves a few words of clarification. The three principles of liberty, equality and fraternity constitute the core of Ambedkar's social philosophy. These very principles are the parameters of any ideal religion as well. Ambedkar does not exempt the Buddhist monks from his reconstruction. Traditionally, a *bhikku* of the Buddhist order was supposed to devote himself to disciplining his own behaviour, speech and mind by following the rules of *Śīla* and meditation. But Ambedkar wishes the monk to play the social role of spreading the understanding of *Dhamma* among the common people, and enlightening on the matters of morality. He found that the monks of Theravād countries like Śri Lanka and elsewhere were not playing their social role properly.

A *bhikku*, for Ambedkar is not an ascetic or recluse. He, according to Ambedkar, would fail as a *bhikku* if he is indifferent to the woes of the mankind. He should be a warrior, who does not avoid fighting when virtue is in danger.

that the harmony consists in the sum total, and not in one note.

Supremacy of God and Efficacy of Prayers

Both Hinduism and Islam accept God as the Supreme and Absolute Lord of the universe, Creator and Sustainer of all creatures. All Muslims and Hindus pray to God and firmly believe and hope that He will answer their prayers. They also believe that He has the power to execute and enforce His will, by which everything in the universe moves. In other words, nothing moves and nothing can move without His will. They are answerable to Him for all their actions, good or bad. They will get reward for their good deeds and punishment for misdeeds. Islam believes in God's reward for good deeds and punishment for bad deeds. Thus declares the *Qur'an*, "Whoever does good deed, he shall be repaid ten-fold; and whoever does evil, he shall be repaid with evil." (5.32). Likewise, Hinduism believes in the law of *karma*. The law of *karma* is the law of cause and effect, that is, 'as you sow so shall you reap'. Truly, one becomes good by good action and bad by bad action (*Brihdaranyaka Upnishad,* 111.2.13).

Islamic *Kalma* that there is no God but Allah and Muhammad is not the Prophet of God means nor should it be interpreted to mean that Allah is the God of Muslims only and none else. Likewise, the words that Muhammad is the Prophet of God do not mean nor it should be interpreted to mean that Muhammad is the only Prophet sent by God. As mentioned above, God has sent Messengers for all people.

As discussed above, the words 'Allah' and 'God' are synonyms. *Allah* is an Arabic word which means God in English, *Ishwar* in Hindi and *Khuda* in Persian and other equivalents in more than 2000 languages of the world, as mentioned above. There is nothing like Hindu God or Muslim God. Those who think so is merely the figment of their imagination.

Basic Moral Values and Responsibilities

Both religions believe in moral values like love, compassion, righteousness, non-violence, justice, forgiveness, tolerance, mercy, moderation in eating, drinking and all walks of life, self-control, brotherhood, amity, friendliness, patience, gratitude, respect to elders, etc. Can anyone lay one's hands on any religious scripture which forbids possession of these attributes? Why to fight then? Why to kill each other? Let the Muslims ponder over the *Quranic* mandate "whoever kills a human life... it is as though he kills all mankind; and whoever saves a life, it is as though he saved all mankind." (6.160). Let the Hindus ponder over the concept of *Ahimsa*, that is, non-injury, non-violence, tolerance, peace, compassion, love towards all creatures.

Conversion and regard for other religions

Both religions do not permit forced conversion from one religion to the other. *Quran* clearly ordains:

There is to be no compulsion in religion. (2.256)

Gandhiji also held the same view: "There is nothing in the Koran to warrant the use of force for conversion." (***The Mind of Gandhi***, p. 100 by R.K. Raghu and V.R. Rao)

Be courteous when you argue with the people of the scriptures, except for those who do evil. Say to them, "We believe in that which has been revealed to us and revealed to you, and our God and your God is One, and to Him do we submit." (29.46). Islam does not specifically recognise some of the religions specifically and explicitly but it is clearly ordained in *Qur'an* that all those who are pious and those who do not indulge in evil deeds deserve all respect, irrespective of the religion they profess. Hindus also believe that each individual has a choice to pursue a path in accordance with his or her inner inclination and religious beliefs and interfering with it would tantamount to taking responsibility for another's salvation and also *karma*.

Doomsday and End of the World, that is Qayamat and Parle

Both the religions believe in the ultimate end and destruction of the world and Almighty's favour to the pious and punishment to the sinners. Both of them believe in hell and heaven, though the concept and terminology adopted for the two may be different. It may be *jannat* and *dozakh* or *nark* and *swarg*.

Importance of Pilgrimage

Followers of both of these religions believe in pilgrimage to their respective holy places known as *Haj* for Muslims and *Yatras* for Hindus.

Help to the Poor

Both the religions provide for help to the poor though the approach or mode of assistance may not technically be the same. In Islam, it is in the form of *Zakat*, a term used in Islamic finance to refer to the obligation that an individual has to donate a certain proportion of his/her wealth each year for charitable purposes.

Likewise almost all Hindu scriptures speak of charity and help to the poor in unequivocal terms. To quote:

Whatever you do, whatever you eat, whatever you offer in sacrifice; whatever charity you give, whatever austerity you practice, do it as an offering to Me.

—(*Gita*: 9.27)

Recitation from scriptures on pious and ceremonial occasions

Recitation from scriptures on pious and ceremonial occasions is a common practice among Hindus and Muslims, such as day-to-day prayers, marriage, death, death anniversaries, house warming ceremonies, etc.

Why Certain Sections of Hindus Put Questions to Indian Muslims about the Following Issues?

Reconstruction of demolished temples, bogey of rapidly rising population of Muslims and the apprehension of their emergence as majority community without proper reference to census figures, declining Hindu population in Pakistan and Bangladesh, conversion, *Madrasa* education, on one hand, states granting recognition and giving financial aid to such institutions and Hindu students also receiving education in these *Madrasas* and getting government jobs and, on the other hand, calling them as centres of "fundamentalism" (an old theological and ecclesiastical term having fallen prey to a narrow interpretation by certain vested interests). However, it is not something new. Words change their meanings with the passage of time. The word 'discourse' as used by Beacon in his essay 'of studies' to mean any discussion has now assumed religious colour and the word 'discourse' is now generally used for religious discourses only). Haj subsidy (now opposed by certain sections of Muslims, too, being not financially viable), remarks to the effect that India had Muslim Presidents, a Sikh Prime Minister and a Christian Defence Minister, why can' it happen in Pakistan or Bangladesh, Muslim MPs and Ministers taking oath in the name of Allah, promotion of ancient languages like Arabic and Persian (Is English a native language?), legal rights to Bangladeshsis to settle and become Indian citizens, when Deepavali and Janmashtami are celebrated at White House, House of Commons, Australian Parliament, etc. why are they not celebrated, in Indian Parliament? (Are Indian Muslims opposed to it?). If Islam and Christianity believe in *Sarva Dharma Samabhava*, why do they go for conversion? Islam and Christianity are political ideologies aimed at grabbing nations through Mullahs and Fathers, concept of 'secular Muslim' is a misnomer, a person can either be secular or a Muslim, and not both, a Muslim (who (believes in the only God (Allah) and not in gods and *devtas*) cannot be secular (believing in many gods); Why Christian missionaries do not go to Muslim-dominated areas and start social service there? Is it because they will not get sufficient return to their 'investment'?; the policies of all political parties are based on vote bank politics aimed at appeasing Muslims, the Constitution has been amended several times to negate the verdicts of the High Courts and Supreme Court? – Shah Bano, unseating of Indira Gandhi, etc., Muslims want to convert India into *Darul Islam* which is at present *Darul Harab* for them.

There is a popular belief that under the Muslim rule forced conversions were the order of the day and that Islam spread through sword. There could be such stray incidents and clean chit cannot be given to wrong-doers. Had it been so, Hindus would have been deprived of their majority status in India during hundreds years of Muslim rule in India. Hindus continued to be the majority population in the Mughal capital Delhi and all over the empire even after five centuries of Muslim rule. Is it not a fact that Muslims ruled Spain for centuries without forcible conversion? Is it not a fact that the percentage of Muslim population in Spain is less than five per cent today? The same picture is that of the Ottoman Empire (between 13th century and 20th century). Were Arabia, Central Asia and Greece as also the Slavic nations not ruled by Turkey between 1500 and 1920? Is it not a fact that Christians lived peacefully in Turkey, Syria, Egypt, etc.

In the changed scenario, Muslims should not be blamed for all types of present-day violence. However, it does not mean that all Muslims are saints but it does not, too, mean that all of them are devils. The same yardstick may be applied to the followers of other religions. As a matter of fact, religion and violence cannot or at least should not go side by side. Both of them are opposed to each other. Blame game may not serve any purpose; it may further aggravate the situation.

Is present generation of Muslims answerable to the deeds or misdeeds of earlier generations? Are Indian Muslims responsible for what is happening in Pakistan or Bangladesh or in any other Muslim country? Why performance of theocratic states is compared to that of a secular state? Was the Indian Constitution imposed on all Indians at the instance of Muslims? Was it not adopted by the people of India as a whole as so mentioned in its Preamble, reproduced below?

"WE THE PEOPLE OF INDIA, having solemnly resolved

to constitute India into a [SOVEREIGN, SOCIALIST,

SECULAR, DEMOCRATIC REPUBLIC] and to secure

to all its citizens: JUSTICE, social, economic and political;

LIBERTY of thought, expression, belief, faith and worship;

EQUALITY of status and of opportunity; and to promote

among them all; FRATERNITY assuring the dignity of

the individual and integrity of the Nation];

IN OUR CONSTITUENT ASSEMBLY this twenty-sixth day of November, 1949, do HEREBY ADOPT, ENACT AND GIVE TO OURSELVES THIS CONSTITUTION."

Was the Preamble of the Constitution drafted by the Muslims for the Muslims or was it drafted by the Hindus for the Hindus? Can Gandhiji, Maulana Azad, Nehru, Bhagat Singh, Chandra Shekhar Azad or Ashfaqullah Khan or a host of many other persons with similar attributes or background be divided on religious lines or can we divide present leadership on these lines? Ideological differences between the people are always appreciable in a democratic state but their patriotism cannot be judged on the strength of these parameters provided such ideologies are not inconsistent with the permissible constitutional and legal parameters. Have Indian Muslims shown any disrespect to Hindu gods and deities? Have Muslim writers and poets not praised them in their writings? Are Pakistani poets not using the word *Ganga* and such expressions in their poetry?

Is *Ganga-Jamuni tehzeeb* (Ganges-Yamuna culture) not an euphemism for the mutually participatory co-existence of Hindu and Muslim culture in Northern India? Have Nawabs of Awadh not been fore-runners of this culture? Are Ustad Bismillah Khan, Anand Narain Mulla, Raghupath Sahai Firaq Gorakhpuri, Anand Mohan Zutshi Gulzar Dehlvi, Sampooran Singh Kalra Gulzar, etc., not uncontested and undeniable symbols of this mixed and composite culture of which we feel proud and shall always.

According to a saying of the Prophet Muhammad(S), Hazrat Adam (AS) had descended on the Indian soil. The Prophet had also proclaimed that he smelt a "fragrance of spirituality" coming from India. Why all of us should not continue to share this fragrance. No one relishes dirty smell. Allama Iqbal, the poet, philosopher and writer of the song *Saare Jahan Se Achcha Hindostan Hamara,* wrote about *Rama:*

Hai Ram Ke wajood Pe Hindostaan ko Naaz,

Ahle Nazar Samjhatein hain Unko Imaame Hind.

(India is proud of Rama and so the wise men. They consider him as *Imame Hind*).

He also wrote:

Khak-e-watan ka mujhko har zarra devta hai

(To me every particle of the country's soil is a deity). Iqbal was not a *Ram Bhakt* but he had full regard for him. Likewise, every Muslim must have high regard for him and the attributes possessed by and attributed to him. To show any disrespect to any deity or religion is against basic tenets of all religions. Religion has own merits and demerits (if misused or interpreted fanatically), but its followers and interpreters should not be allowed to surpass *Lakshman rekha* (its domain or limit, transgression of which may have dire consequences). **Those with jaundiced eyes and masked faces, whosoever they may be, shall ever remain off the track. There are many such gems which have been forgotten in the din of communalism.**

Na Hindu Bura hai, Na Mussalman bura hai

Burai Pe ajaye to Insan bura hai

(No one is bad, neither a Hindu nor a Muslim, their deeds and misdeeds are the parameters of their vice and virtue).

It is the fanatics who have eroded the trust between these two communities which lived and shared each other's joy and sorrow for centuries together and the global situation is adding fuel to the fire.

It will not be out of place to reproduce here certain portions of a dialogue between former RSS Chief K. S. Sudarshan and Maulana Abdul Hameed Nomani of Jamiat-e-Ulema-e-Hind that have a direct bearing on the subject:

In 2004, he (Sudershan Ji) had felt the need for a dialogue with the Muslims as the mutual misunderstandings could not be removed without it. For that purpose, he chose the Jamiat-e-Ulema-e- Hind.

At the outset, he raised the point that there were many hurdles in the Hindu-Muslim unity. And first of them was the question in what category the Muslims kept the Hindus. Giving reference to Syed Sulaiman Nadvi's book, "*Indo-Arab Relations and the Seerat of the Prophet*", and other books, he said that according to the Islamic *Shariah*, mankind was divided in four categories—*Mumin, kafir, ahl-e-kitab* and *shib'h ahl-e-kitab* (believers, non-believers, people with the divine book and people who were like all-e-kitab). "Now the question is", he said, "in which category do you people keep the Hindus?" From his questions one could get the line of Sudarshan's study. .. Quoting different references I (Maulana Nomani) made it clear to him that our jurisprudential scholars had replied to his question much earlier saying that the Hindus of India came under the category of Shib'h-e-ahl-e-kitab. When this question was raised during the reign of Muhammad Bin Quasim, Khwaja Hasan Basri and other scholars had replied this to the query of Hajjaj Bin Yousuf. While Syed Sulaiman Nadvi has raised the issue in his book '*Seeratun Nabi and Indo-Arab Relations*' the answer is also given.

I (the said Maulana) also threw the salvo asking him in which category he put Indian Muslims under his religious point of view and what his ideal was on which we should take the dialogue further.

Sudarshan seemed perturbed by my (Abdul Hameed Nomani's) questions... I (Abdul Hameed Nomani) also told him...They (particularly) the Muslims of Indian origin have never rejected Ram and Krishna. Why then is the issue of recognising them as their ancestors raked up?

(*Source*: *Azad Hind,* Urdu Daily, Kolkata, Nov. 1, 2012).

Justice Mr. Markandey Katju, former Judge, Supreme Court of India, presently Chairperson, Press Council of India, while delivering a lecture at Jamia Millia Islamia on 8.2.2011, had said that intellectuals are the eyes of society, and without intellectuals a society is blind... and a heavy responsibility lies on the intellectuals to advance forward. He also referred to a judgement delivered by him[1] in which he had mentioned that India is broadly a country of immigrants, and this explains its tremendous diversity...India is a country of old immigrants where people have been coming in for ten thousand years or so. Probably about 92 per cent people living in India today are descendants of immigrants, who came mainly from the North-West, and to a lesser extent from the North-East. In order to substantiate his claim, he also quoted a couplet of great Urdu poet Firaq Gorakhpuri who had also described this situation in these words:

"Sar zamin-e-Hind par aqwaam-e-alam ke firaq

Quafile guzarte gae Hindustan banta gaya."

(Caravans of people kept coming to India from various parts of the world and they became its integral part).

Why to arouse passions by raising bogus issues, particularly about religious teachings in *madrasas*, communalism, etc.? If *madrasas* are factories of terrorism why they are being financed by the states? Have those running these institutions ever been indicted? Can the follies of a few individuals be attributed to their religion they profess or the institutions in which they are studying? Can such a yardstick be applied to all institutions because such stray incidents may take place anywhere? Do all state reports reveal that Muslims are responsible for all communal riots in India? Have Indian Muslims been instrumental to the inclusion of Article 370 in the Constitution? Have Indian Muslims stopped or can they stop the Supreme Court in giving various verdicts to the effect that Article 44 (Uniform Civil Code) be implemented only if there is a move from the Muslims? Is cleansing of Muslims or any other community whatsoever possible in this civilised world? Has the ouster of Kashmiri Pandits been hailed by any sane group of people? Is there any Muslim or any Muslim group in the fool's paradise thinking that he/she or they will be able to re-establish Muslim rule in India again or that they should strive therefor? Is it not a fact that Muslims are aspiring only for social justice and relatively equal treatment and nothing else? Are they not aware of the saying "Do what the Romans do"? But our Hindu brothers, instead of condemning them, must realise that Muslims have some religious compulsions and they cannot compromise in certain matters because of these compulsions. For example, it may not be possible for any devout Muslim to bow his head before any deity. Does it mean that he is a bad Muslim? Certainly not. He may be a pious person who may be much ahead of others in helping his Hindu neighbour, if need be. Likewise, a Hindu gentleman may not eat food cooked in a Muslim mess apprehending that it might have been cooked in the utensils used for preparing some food which is not acceptable to a devout Hindu. It does not mean that he is a bad Hindu. In the same way, a Muslim may avoid taking food at a place where pork is being served. Some of my Hindu friends are non-vegetarians but they do not force their wives to prepare non-veg food so that their religious feelings are not hurt.

Slaughtering of certain animals is permissible on ceremonial occasions under municipal laws but if someone is living in a Hindu dominated society or his neighbours get hurt by such action, the animal may be slaughtered somewhere else even if his neigbours do not object so that their religious feelings are not hurt. No Muslim or any Muslim organisation is stretching its hands towards any foreign power even in distress and compelling situations. Our media and intellectuals have now come in open to champion their cause and advocate their case as strongly rather more strongly as their religious fraternity could do.

Indian Muslims are fed up with reference to Babar as invader. How the present-day generation of Muslims, most of them being converts, is answerable for that. Some of the historians are of the view (though the views may be conflicting and divergent and all the groups may not accept them) that many Hindu rulers had invited the Muslim invaders, including Babar, in order to settle scores with local rulers and one ruling Muslim dynasty fought against another ruling Muslim dynasty. When Babar invaded India, Ibrahim Lodhi was ruling over India and he was invited to defeat the Lodhi ruler by Rajput rulers. We should not see all these events with religious angle. The historians maintain that there have been serious differences between the rulers following the same religion and these differences resulted in hostilities and conflicts between them. Muslims fought against Muslims and Hindu rulers fought against Hindu rulers. If Aurangzeb was a hardliner for Hindus, he was equally so for his own community. On the one hand, there are instances of his imposing *jazia* but, on the other, there are examples of his giving land and money to temples for construction. At the same time, he is known for ordering execution of some Muslim saints and persons challenging his decisions. He was also known for his disciplined life and honesty. Here I remember the narration of one of my friends, possessing Ph.D. degree in history, regarding his interview in Union Public Service Commission for the post of Senior Administrative Officer (civil) in Ministry of Defence. The first question put to him was: Which of the Mughal rulers was the best? He replied without hesitation -Aurangzeb. The concerned member of the board asked him, may be surprisingly, HOW? His instant reply was "Sir, he was a very honest and disciplined person and every person serving in a defence organisation must possess these two attributes". Hats off to that Board! He was recommended for appointment. Thus our thinking and approach to things makes all the difference.

Our purpose is not to glorify or condemn any one; our purpose is to present things in such a way that the tension between these two communities is reduced, if not eliminated instantaneously. Likewise, in a meeting of a UN recognised NGO and a reliable think tank, one of the office bearers and a popular personality known for his liberal outlook was noticed complaining that some of the deserving Muslim candidates, being at the top of the merit/seniority list, were ignored for some prestigious posts though it is generally complained that Muslim candidates are not available. His complaint could be genuine but there are other examples, too, which present a different story. There are many examples when a Muslim candidate had been selected against a single post when all other candidates were Hindus/non-Muslims. But it does not mean that there is no discrimination against Muslims. But at the same time, discrimination is not limited to Muslims only. Even persons belonging to other communities, including majority community, fall prey to it at the hands of those prejudiced against various sections of people on various grounds, though our laws do not permit discrimination on any ground whatsoever. But all of us have to come out of this vicious circle. There are certain Hindus who like and share the joy and grief of their Muslim friends but they do not like Muslims as a community. Same is the situation on the other side. Lack of interaction, childhood briefing, family background, dysfunctional families, stereo-type mentality, societal and political compulsions, never to forget the past mentality and other prejudices are responsible for it. But time is a great healing factor. In communal holocaust of 1947, could any Muslim with whatever views imagine that India will have Muslim Presidents (Heads of State) and Chief Justices of India or will they get prestigious awards or that crores of Muslims shall be able to live in India or that after 1984 riots Sikhs would once again become an integral part of the Indian populace as they were before 1984.

Hate writings, unilateral approach, perpetual malice and rigid attitude of both the communities may prove to be non-remedial cancer in the long run. Prevention is better than cure and what cannot be cured must be endured till we reach the ideal situation. When to see backward, why it should be confined to past 800 years' checkered history. Even before Muslims' entry into India, there were hundreds of wars in the country and Hindus killed Hindus. The *Mahabharat* was not a Muslim plan. Invading Muslim armies killed Indian Muslim armies. Who has not heard the name of Nadir Shah? Are Naxalites and Maoists Muslims? Likewise, many Muslims were killed by Muslims in Kashmir. Killers and robbers and those indulged in looting and arson, whosoever they may be, should not be addressed by religion. They are the misguided people or persons with criminal tendencies. Common people are living with each other peacefully.

Let the fanatics and politicians not arouse their passion for getting dividends out of it. Why don't politicians realise that there are larger issues to be taken care of than religious extremism? They should focus on social and economic issues and refrain from using their energy for fanatic and emotional exercises. There are many other issues worth taking up, such as crumbling infrastructure, corruption, poverty, illiteracy, inflation, rising prices, slow rate of growth, national security, etc.,

Quotations on Religious Harmony

Mahatma Gandhi, Father of the Indian Nation

"Unity does not mean political unity which may be imposed. It means an unbreakable heart unity. The first thing essential for achieving such a unity is for every person, whatever his religion may be, to represent in his own person Hindu, Muslim, Christian, Zoroastrian, Jew, etc. In order to realise this, every person will cultivate personal friendship with persons representing faiths other than his own. He should have the same regard for the other faiths as he has for his own."

"Let us forget all thoughts of, I am Hindu, you a Muslim, or I am a Gujarati, you a Madrasi, let us think, I and mine in a common Indian Nationality. We shall be free only when a large number of our people are determined to swim or sink together."

Pandit Jawahar Lal Nehru, the Builder of Modern India

"The past of India, with its cultural variety and greatness, was a common heritage of all the Indian people, Hindu, Muslim, Christian and others, and their ancestors had helped to build it." (***Discovery of India***, p. 341).

Sardar Vallabh Bhai Patel, the Iron man of India had also advised the people of India in a post-partition public address at Lucknow:

'Let us all, who belong to India, swim or sink together.'

Maulana Abul Kalam Azad, the father figure of the Indian National Movement and an icon of secular nationalism

Maulana Abul Kalam Azad started a weekly journal in Urdu called *Al Hilal* to increase the revolutionary recruits amongst the Muslims. *Al-Hilal* played an important role in forging Hindu-Muslim unity after the bad blood created between the two communities in the aftermath of Morley-Minto reforms. *Al Hilal* became a revolutionary mouthpiece ventilating extremist views.

Regarding the personality of Maulana Abul Kalam Azad, former President of India, Dr. S. Radhakrishnan, had remarked:

"We are too near the tragedy even to make a proper assessment of the great services rendered by Maulana Azad to our freedom movement and to our progress thereafter. He was a great scholar; a self-sacrificing patriot and a statesman. One great thing for which our people have to remember Maulana Azad is his work for India's unity."

(***Maulana Abul Kalam Azad***, by Arsh Malsiani, Government of India publication, 1988) (Please refer to his historic speech delivered at Jama Masjid, Delhi after partition quoted in chapter 1).

Reference

1. Kailas and Others vs. State of Maharashtra, 2011(1) JT 19.

6

Constitutional Mandate for Religious Harmony and National Integration

Minorities exist wherever there is a majority. Protection of minorities means protection of human rights. The degree of a nation being civilised is measured by its treatment of the minorities and other weaker sections of the society.

The Indian Constitution provides full protection to the religious and linguistic minorities without specifying the minorities. Prior to the analysis of these provisions it would be pertinent to go through conceptual history of the term 'minority'. After the partition of India on religious grounds, a new State (Pakistan) was carved out. During the pre-partition days, Maulana Abul Kalam Azad, the father figure of the Indian National Movement, whose secular credentials do not require any proof or testimony, firmly believed in one nation and one community, that is, the Indian Nation and the Indian Community. According to him, there was nothing like a minority in the Indian polity. He, while addressing Congress Session at Ramgarh in 1940, had made it clear in unequivocal terms that nothing was more misunderstood than the Muslims were being called a minority community in India. He advised them not to have any doubts or suspicion regarding their rights in undivided India. To Maulana, India meant only unpartitioned India. The Maulana had expressed these views at a time when the Constituent Assembly, of which he was a member, was discussing incorporation of provisions for affording protection to the minorities. The original proposal of the Advisory Committee in the Constituent Assembly had recommended that the minorities in every unit shall be protected in respect of their language, script and culture and no laws or regulations may be enacted that may operate oppressively or prejudicially in this respect. It is another thing that the word 'minority' was substituted by the words 'section of citizens'. Motilal Nehru Report, 1928 had expressed the view that protection should be afforded to the minorities but this Report, too, did not define the term 'minority'. Likewise, the Sapru Report, 1945 had used the words 'Minority Commission' but did not define the term. The U.N. Sub-Commission on Prevention of Discrimination and Protection of Minorities has defined 'minority' as one including only those non-dominant groups in a population which possess and wish to preserve stable, ethnic, religious or linguistic traditions or characteristics markedly different from those of the population. It also mentions that such minorities should properly include a number of persons sufficient by themselves to preserve such traditions or characteristics, and that such minorities must be loyal and faithful to the State of which they are nationals. Article 27 of the International Covenant on Civil and Political Rights provides that in those States in which ethnic, religious or linguistic minorities exist, persons belonging to such minorities shall not be denied the right, in community with the other members of their group, to enjoy their own culture, to profess and practise their own religion, or to use their own language but the term 'minority' has not been defined in this Convention too.

It was after 43 years of the enforcement of the Constitution that by a notification issued in 1993 under the National Commission for Minorities Act, 1992, the Muslims, Christians, Sikhs, Buddhists and Parsi Zoroastrians were notified as the 'minorities' at the national level for the purposes of the Act. In TMA Pai's case (2002), the Supreme Court has held that linguistic and religious minorities are covered by the expression 'minority' under Article 30 of the Constitution. Since reorganisation of the states in India has been on linguistic lines, therefore, for the purpose of determining the minority, the unit will be the state and not the whole of India. Thus, religious and linguistic minorities, who have been put at par in Article 30, have to be considered state-wise. In the same case, the Supreme Court has dealt with the concepts of equality and secularism and given a clear picture of the implementation mechanism. To quote:

'Our country is often depicted as a person in the form of "Bharat Mata, the Mother India".

The people of India are regarded as her children with their welfare being in her heart. Like any loving mother, the welfare of the family is of paramount importance for her. For a healthy family, it is important that each member is strong and healthy. But then, all members do not have the same constitution, whether physical and/

or mental. For harmonious and healthy growth, it is but natural for the parents, and the mother in particular, to give more attention and food to the weaker child so as to help him/her become stronger. Giving extra food and attention and ensuring private tuition to help in his/her studies will, in a sense, amount to giving the weaker child preferential treatment. Just as lending physical support to the aged and the infirm, or providing a special diet, cannot be regarded as unfair or unjust, similarly, conferring certain rights on a special class, for good reasons, cannot be considered inequitable. All the people of India are not alike, and that is why, preferential treatment to a special section of the society is not frowned upon. Article 30 is a special right conferred on the religious and linguistic minorities because of their numerical handicap and to instill in them a sense of security and confidence, even though the minorities cannot be *per se* regarded as weaker sections or underprivileged segments of the society. The one billion population of India consists of six main ethnic groups and fifty-two major tribes; six major religions and 6,400 castes and sub-castes; eighteen major languages and 1,600 minor languages and dialects. The essence of secularism in India can best be depicted if a relief map of India is made in mosaic, where the aforesaid one billion people are the small pieces of marble that go into the making of a map. Each person, whatever his/her language, caste, religion has his/her individual identity, which has to be preserved, so that when pieced together it goes to form a depiction with the different geographical features of India. These small pieces of marble, in the form of human beings, which may individually be dissimilar to each other, when placed together in a systematic manner, produce the beautiful map of India. Each piece, like a citizen of India, plays an important part in making of the whole. The variations of the colours as well as different shades of the same colour in a map is the result of these small pieces of different shades and colours of marble, but even when one small piece of marble is removed, the whole map of India would be scarred, and the beauty would be lost. Each of the people of India has an important place in the formation of the nation. Each piece has to retain its own colour. By itself, it may be an insignificant stone, but when placed in a proper manner, goes into the making of a full picture of India in all its different colours and hues. A citizen of India stands in a similar position. The Constitution recognises the differences among the people of India, but it gives equal importance to each of them, their differences notwithstanding, for only then can there be a unified secular nation. Recognising the need for the preservation and retention of different pieces that go into the making of a whole nation, the Constitution, while maintaining, *inter alia*, the basic principle of equality, contains adequate provisions that ensure the preservation of these different pieces. The essence of secularism in India is the recognition and preservation of the different types of people, with diverse languages and different beliefs, and placing them together so as to form a whole and united India. Articles 29 and 30 do not more than seek to preserve the differences that exist, and at the same time, unite the people to form one strong nation."

Religious harmony and national integration, as contemplated in the Constitution, is the need of the hour but religious fanaticism, which is wrongly described as religious fundamentalism, has plagued the global atmosphere. In the Charter of the United Nations, the nations of the world had determined to reaffirm faith in fundamental human rights, in the dignity and worth of the human person and to practise tolerance and live together in peace with one another as good neighbours. But even in the 21st century, divisive forces and religious fanatics are raising their ugly head. Such elements are bent upon polluting the atmosphere. They are demolishing religious places, desecrating deities, and resorting to loot and arson, besides killing innocent people by applying most inhuman methods. Even women and children are burnt alive.

Communalism is the basic feature of the so-called fundamentalism, whereas religious harmony and national integration are the basic features of the Indian Constitution. Religion is a deep and moving source of self-identity and, sometimes, it is noticed that group sentiments can be quickly aroused on religious grounds and this noble sentiment is turned into hatred and fanaticism and, as stated above, such communal elements resort to irrational acts. Religious appeal is so appealing that even in 1940 when Stalin was fighting against Hitler's forces and was in trouble decided to appeal to the religious sentiments and religious history of the Soviet people to arouse their patriotic feelings though he was an atheist. Even Saddam Hussain, who headed a country the Constitution of which is/was secular, appealed to the Muslim world to help him in the name of religion. However, it is worth appreciating that in the Indian struggle for freedom people professing different religions participated actively. Those who believed in Two-nation theory and apprehended backlash from opposite quarter migrated to Pakistan and those who believed in One-nation theory and one people, the people of India, as also those who reconciled to the changed situation, preferred to stay in India hoping that all of them will be treated as sons of the soil and shall also be treated at par in all walks of life, an expectation yet to be fulfilled, as so confirmed by Sachar Committee and Justice Ranganath Mishra Commission.

The root cause of communalism is the faulty education about other religions and members of other communities. The members of different communities get unbalanced by a communal group label, such as Hindu, Muslim, Sikh or Christian, etc., and tend to think irrationally that only members of their own community are always right or just and others are wrong. In that way, they tilt in favour of their own community and discriminate against members of other communities. It is absolutely an irrational approach.

As a matter of fact, religion is not the root cause of the communal problem but it is the misuse of the religion that leads to it. According to Dr. S. Radhakrishnan, religion is a dynamic process, a renewed effort of the creative impulses working through exceptional individuals and seeking to uplift humankind to a new level. But unfortunately, what we are noticing today is that we are not uplifting the humankind but we are bringing the humankind to the lowest level by misusing the religion and doing what every religion prohibits to do. In the changed socio-political scenario, the intellectuals have also lost their voice. It is high time that the intellectuals of our country must come forward to undertake the responsibility of creating congenial atmosphere in the country in which all of us may live in peace as brothers and sisters as was expected by the founding fathers of our Constitution. Article 51A of the

Constitution provides that it shall be the duty of every citizen of India to abide by the Constitution and respect its ideals and institutions, to cherish and follow the noble ideas which inspired our national struggle for freedom, to uphold and protect the sovereignty, unity and integrity of India, to value and preserve the rich heritage of our composite culture and to develop the scientific temper, humanism and the spirit of enquiry and reform, and to strive towards the excellence in all spheres of individual and collective activity so that the nation constantly rises to higher levels of endeavour and achievement. Thus anyone, who does not abide by the Constitution and does not respect its ideals and institutions, strikes at the Constitution itself. It is an act unbecoming of a citizen or national of a civilised country.

The founding fathers of the Constitution were equally worried about the religious harmony in the country. The Constituent Assembly, set-up in view of Cabinet Mission Plan, had also suggested that an Advisory Committee on the rights of the citizens, minorities, tribals and for excluded areas be set up. Thus, the Cabinet Mission Plan itself separately categorised citizens as minorities, tribals and the excluded areas. The Advisory Committee was constituted and its Report was submitted prior to the framing of the Constitution. The framers of the Constitution protected the rights of various minorities throughout the country. In Ahmedabad, *St. Xavier's College Society* v. *State of Gujarat* (AIR 1974 SC 1389) it was held:-

"There is no mysticism in the secular character of the State. Secularism is neither anti-God nor pro-God. It treats alike the devout, the agnostic and atheist. It eliminates God from the matters of the State and ensures that no one shall be discriminated against on the ground of religion."

Constitutional Provisions for Protection of Minorities

Part-III of the Constitution of India, if acted upon in true letter and spirit, is a complete charter of human rights. The provisions contained in this part provide for complete fool-proof protective cover to the minorities. Articles reproduced below bear testimony thereto:

Article 14 provides that the State shall not deny to any person equality before law or equal protection of laws within the territory of India. The doctrine of equality before law follows from the concept of the English 'Rule of Law'. Jennings in his book titled '*Law and the Constitution*' has defined the doctrine as under

"Equality before the means that among equals the law should be equal and should be equally administered that like should be treated alike."

All the articles in Part-III of the Constitution guaranteeing Fundamental Rights and freedoms are, in general, equally applicable to the minorities. However, some of these articles have specially been incorporated for the protection of the minorities.

Article 15 of the Constitution provides that the State shall not discriminate against any citizen on grounds only of religion, race, caste, sex, place of birth or any of them and that no citizen shall, on grounds only of religion, race, caste, sex, place of birth or any of them, be subject to any disability, liability, restriction or condition with regard to access to shops, public restaurants, hotels and places of public entertainment or the use of wells, tanks, bathing ghats, roads and places of public resort maintained wholly or partly out of State funds or dedicated to the use of general public. But, at the same time, Clauses three and four of this Article provide that nothing in this article shall prevent the State from making any special provision for women and children and for the advancement of any socially and educationally backward classes of citizens or for the Scheduled Castes and the Scheduled Tribes. It means that reasonable discrimination which may more rationally be described as reasonable classification is always permissible and this is the reason that the Constitution has incorporated special provisions for the protection of Scheduled Castes, Scheduled Tribes, socially and educationally backward classes of citizens, minorities and other categories of persons.

Article 16 provides for equality of opportunity in matters of public employment. It reads as under:

(1) There shall be equality of opportunity for all citizens in matters relating to employment or appointment to any office under the State.

(2) No citizen shall, on grounds only of religion, race, caste, sex, descent, place of birth, residence or any of them, be ineligible for, or discriminated against in respect of, any employment or office under the State.

(3) Nothing in this article shall prevent Parliament from making any law prescribing, in regard to a class or classes of employment or appointment to an office (under the Government of, or any local or other authority within a State or Union territory, any requirement as to residence within that State or

Union Territory) prior to such employment or appointment.

(4) Nothing in this article shall prevent the State from making any provision for the reservation of appointments or posts in favour of any backward class of citizens which, in the opinion of the State, is not adequately represented in the services under the State.

Articles 19 to 22 guarantee various freedoms, such as, protection of certain rights regarding freedom of speech, etc., protection in respect of conviction for offences, protection of life and personal liberty and protection against arrest and detention in certain cases and all these freedoms are available to the minorities in the manner the same are available to the majority community and so is the case of right against exploitation as provided in Articles 23 and 24.

Articles 25 to 28 of the Constitution preserve and protect the freedom of all religions professed in the country.

Article 25 guarantees freedom of conscience and free profession, practise and propagation of religion. It reads as under:

"(1) Subject to public order, morality and health and to the other provisions of this part, all persons are equally entitled to freedom of conscience and the right freely to profess, practise and propagate religion.

(2) Nothing in this article shall affect the operation of any existing law or prevent the State from making any law-

(a) regulating or restricting any economic, financial, political or other secular activity which may be associated with religious practice;

(b) providing for social welfare and reform or the throwing open of Hindu religious institutions of a public character to all classes and sections of Hindus.

Explanation 1 – The wearing and carrying of *kirpans* shall be deemed to be included in the profession of the Sikh religion.

Explanation II — In sub-clause (b) of Clause (2), the reference to Hindus shall be construed as including a reference to persons professing the Sikh, Jaina or Buddhist religion, and the reference to Hindu religious institutions shall be construed accordingly".

A plain reading of the article indicates that the freedom granted under this article is subject to certain curbs i.e. subject to public order, morality and health. In other words, the liberty granted under this article is not unfettered as unfettered liberty may be granted only when the law of jungle is in operation. Such sort of curbs and fetters are required to curb religious fanaticism. It is not only in the Indian Constitution that such a rider has been applied. Even in the most advanced nations of the world and those who claim to be the advocates and champions of human rights and in whose constitutions it is provided that the religious freedom is an inviolable right, have put such curbs in their constitutions and rightly so because a civilised society can never permit persons belonging to the majority community or the minority community to resort to religious fanaticism and hurt feelings of each other.

Article 26 grants freedom to manage religious affairs. It reads as under :

"Subject to public order, morality and health, every religious denomination or any section thereof shall have the right –

(a) to establish and maintain institutions for religious and charitable purposes;

(b) to manage its own affairs in matters of religion;

(c) to own and acquire moveable and immoveable property; and

(d) to administer such property in accordance with law."

Article 27 grants freedom as to payment of taxes for promotion of any particular religion. It reads as under:

"No person shall be compelled to pay any taxes, the proceeds of which are specifically appropriated in payment of expenses for the promotion or maintenance of any particular religion or religious denomination."

Article 28 grants freedom as to attendance at religious instruction or religious worship in certain educational institutions. It reads as under:

"No religious instruction shall be provided in any educational institution wholly maintained out of State funds.

(2) Nothing in Cl. (1) shall apply to an educational institution which is administered by the State but has been established under any endowment or trust which requires that religious instruction shall be imparted in such institution.

No person attending any educational institution recognised by the State or receiving aid out of State funds shall be required to take part in any religious instruction that may be imparted in such institution or to attend any religious worship that may be conducted in such institution or in any premises attached thereto unless such person or, if such person is a minor, his guardian has given his consent thereto."

Article 29: Protection of interests of minorities—(1) Any section of the citizens residing in the territory of India or any part thereof having a distinct language, script or culture of its own shall have the right to conserve the same.

(2) No citizen shall be denied admission into any educational institution maintained by the State or receiving aid out of State funds on grounds only of religion, race, caste, language or any of them.

Article 29(2) applies to minorities as well as to non-minorities, when other qualifications being equal the religion, race, caste, language of a citizen shall not be a ground of preference or disability.

Article 30: Right of minorities to establish and administer educational institutions— (1) All minorities, whether based on religion or language, shall have the right to establish and administer educational institutions of their choice.

(1A) In making any law providing for the compulsory acquisition of any property of an educational institution established and administered by a minority, referred to in clause (1), the State shall ensure that the amount fixed by or determined under such law for the acquisition of such property is such as would not restrict or abrogate the right guaranteed under that clause.

(2) The State shall not, in granting aid to educational institutions, discriminate against any educational

institution on the ground that it is under the management of a minority, whether based on religion or language.

Besides the Constitution of India, various other laws also contain provisions with a bearing on minority rights.

Sections 153A, 153, 295, 295A, 296, 297 and 298 have been included in the Indian Penal Code so that religious feelings of any citizen are not hurt and communal harmony is preserved in its true sense. These sections are reproduced as under:

"153A. Promoting enmity between different groups of religion, race, place of birth, residence, language, etc., and doing acts prejudicial to maintenance of harmony – (1) –

(a) by words, either spoken or written, or by signs or by visible representations or otherwise, promotes or attempts to promote, on grounds of religion, race, place of birth, residence, language, caste or community or any other ground whatsoever, disharmony or feelings of enmity, hatred, or ill-will between different religious, racial, language or regional groups or castes, or communities; or

(b) commits any act which is prejudicial to the maintenance of harmony between different religious, racial, language or regional groups or castes or communities, and which disturbs or is likely to disturb the public tranquility, or

(c) organises any movement, drill or other similar activity intending that the participants in such activity shall use or be trained to use criminal force or violence or knowing it to be likely that the participants in such activity will use or be trained to use criminal force or violence or participates in such activity intending to use or be trained to use criminal force or violence or knowing it to be likely that the participants in such activity will use or be trained to use criminal force or violence, against any religious, racial, language or regional group or caste or community and such activity for any reason whatsoever causes or is likely to cause fear or alarm or a feeling of insecurity amongst members of such religious, racial, language or regional group or caste or community,

Shall be punished with imprisonment which may extend to three years, or with fine, or with both.

Offence committed in place of worship, etc. – (2) whoever commits an offence specified in sub-section (1) in any place of worship or any assembly engaged in the performance of religious worship or religious ceremonies, shall be punished with imprisonment which may extend to five years and shall also be liable to fine.

153B. Imputations, assertion prejudicial to national integration – (1) whoever, by words either spoken or written or by signs or by visible representations or otherwise, -

(a) makes or publishes any imputation that any class of persons cannot, by reason of their being members of any religious, racial, language or regional group or caste or community, bear true faith and allegiance to the Constitution of India as by law established or uphold the sovereignty and integrity of India, or

(b) asserts, counsels, advises, propagates or publishes that any class of persons shall, by reason of their being members of any religious, racial, language or regional group or caste or community, be denied or deprived of their rights as citizens of India, or

(c) makes or publishes any assertion, counsel, plea or appeal concerning the obligation of any class of persons, by reason of their being members of any religious, racial, language or regional group or caste or community, and such assertion, counsel, plea or appeal causes or is likely to cause disharmony or feelings of enmity or hatred or ill-will between such members and other persons,

Shall be punished with imprisonment which may extend to three years, or with fine or with both.

(2) Whoever commits an offence specified in sub-section (1) in any place of worship or in any assembly engaged in the performance of religious worship or religious ceremonies, shall be punished with imprisonment which may extend to five years and shall also be liable to fine.

295. Injuring or defiling place of worship with intent to insult the religion of any class - Whoever destroys, damages or defiles any place of worship, or any object held sacred by any class of persons with the intention of thereby insulting the religion of any class of persons or with the knowledge that any class of person is likely to consider such destruction, damage or defilement, as an insult to their religion, shall be punished with imprisonment of either description for a term which may extend to two years, or with fine, or with both.

295A. Deliberate and malicious acts intended to outrage religious feelings of any class by insulting its religion or religious beliefs – Whoever, with deliberate and malicious intention of outraging the religious feelings of any class of citizens of India, by words, either spoken or written or by signs or by visible representations or otherwise insults or attempts to insult the religion or the religious beliefs of that class, shall be punished with imprisonment of either description for a term which may extend to three years or with fine, or with both.

296. Disturbing religious assembly – Whoever voluntarily causes disturbance to any assembly lawfully engaged in the performance of religious worship, or religious ceremonies, shall be punished with imprisonment of either description for a term which may extend to one year, or with fine, or with both.

297. Trespassing on burial places, etc. Whoever with intention of wounding the feelings of any person or of insulting the religion of any person, or with the knowledge that the feelings of any person are likely to be wounded, or that the religion of any person is likely to be insulted thereby, commits any trespass in any place of worship or on any place of sculpture, or any place set apart for the performance of funeral rites or as a depository for the remains of the dead, or offers any indignity to any human corpse or causes disturbance to any person assembled for the performance of funeral ceremonies,

Shall be punished with imprisonment of either description for a term which may extend to one year, or with fine, or with both.

298. Uttering words, etc., with deliberate intent to wound religious feelings – Whoever, with the deliberate intention of wounding the religious feelings of any person, utters any word or makes

> any sound in the hearing of that person or making any gesture in the sight of that person or places, any object in the sight of that person, shall be punished with imprisonment of either description for a term which may extend to one year, or with fine, or with both.

Thus, the law is perfect but the nation is yet to attain perfection.

India has been successfully maintaining its unity from day one of its independence, but the growing communal conflict in India may make one feel as if the unity of the country is in jeopardy today. Mistrust amongst various communities is rising and it is to be checked with a firm hand. As regards the Muslim community, it is the biggest minority community in India and the way it behaves and is treated, sets the communal temper in our country. There is a section of the society in India which looks upon Muslims still in some way foreign to India. These people forget that they are the sons and daughters of the same soil and the same country. They had made a conscientious choice to stay in India in 1947. They preferred secular state to an Islamic state. They are to be rewarded for it and not punished. It will not be wrong to say that majority of the Indian Muslims of partitioned India were also secular as most of them preferred to stay in India. Another important factor which many of us are ignoring in the changed scenario is that the Muslim clergy was by and large more secular than those who had received western education. It is common knowledge that Dar-ul-Uloom, Deoband had whole-heartedly supported the freedom movement. With this background, there is no cogent reason for treating Indian Muslims as second rate citizens, may be by a section of the people. *Bharat Mata*, which they (Indian Muslims) call Mather-I-Hind, is as sacred to them as it is to the majority community or any other minority community. Communal harmony cannot be achieved by fighting or finding fault with each other or criticising each other's religions. It can be achieved only through positive cooperation of all communities and sincere efforts by the State. Good and bad are not to be treated at par. There should be an objective exercise to separate chaff from the grain so that innocent people are not penalised and they are not subject to any inhuman and derogatory treatment and furthermore their human rights that are enshrined in the international covenants and the Constitution of India are not violated.

At the same time, it is also equally important that all minorities, whether Muslims, Christians, Sikhs or Parsis, must not do anything that hurts the feelings of the majority community. Communal harmony is a reciprocal concept. Do good to others, only then they will do good to you. It is the constitutional duty of the minority communities to conduct themselves in such a manner that they earn the trust and confidence of the majority community. They must realise that the religious feelings of the majority community are as sacred to them as their feelings are to them. They cannot bulldoze the majority community by their irresponsible behaviour.

7

Role of Clerics in Hindu-Muslim Unity

Religious and spiritual leaders have a special responsibility to maintain peace on earth and that, too, at a time when humanity stands at a critical juncture in history calling for strong moral and spiritual leadership to help set a new direction for the society in which well-being of the human family gets top priority. It is more so in a religiously sensitive country like ours. They have a commitment to global peace, too, though all of us know that if religions, on one hand, have contributed to the peace of the world but, on the other hand, religions have also been used rather misused to create division between different groups of people and fuel hostilities. Our present-day world is plagued by violence, terrorism, war and destruction, sometimes perpetrated in the name of religion.

An interdependent religious society like ours requires agreement on fundamental ethical and moral values without which there would be chaos and disorder in the society that may result in armed conflict. No individual, group or nation can any longer live in Ivory Tower of isolation or as an isolated microcosm in our interdependent world which we call a global village and believe that the whole of humankind is a single nation or a single family. We must realise that we are a part of the civilised society and our every action has an impact on our fellow beings and the emerging global community. We must realise that there can be no real peace until all groups and communities acknowledge the cultural and religious diversity of the human family in a spirit of mutual respect and understanding, particularly in a country like India which is known for its unity in diversity and its *Ganga-Jamuna tehzeeb* (Ganges-Yamuna culture, an euphemism for the mutually participatory co-existence of Hindu and Muslim culture). A true culture of peace must be founded upon the cultivation of the inner dimension of peace, which is the heritage of the religious and spiritual traditions, the example being the said Ganges-Yamuna culture. Such traditions are the core source of the realisation of a better life for the human family and all life on earth and ensure a dignified human existence.

It was for the first time in the history that at the dawn of the new millennium religious and spiritual leaders from various religious traditions, and from all regions of the world, met at the Millennium World Peace Summit in the United Nations to pledge themselves to work for peace. Among the religions represented at the Millennium World Peace Summit were: Bahaiis, Buddhism, Christianity, Confucianism, Hinduism, Indigenous Peoples, Islam, Jainism, Judaism, Shinto, Sikhism, Taoism, and Zoroas-trianism. Religious and spiritual leaders representing these religions signed a document known as "Commitment to Global Peace" and resolved to:

1. Collaborate with the United Nations and all men and women of goodwill locally, regionally and globally in the pursuit of peace in all its dimensions;

2. Lead humanity by word and deed in a renewed commitment to ethical and spiritual values, which include a deep sense of respect for all life and for each person's inherent dignity and right to live in a world free of violence;

3. Manage and resolve non-violently the conflicts generated by religious and ethnic differences, and to condemn all violence committed in the name of religion while seeking to remove the roots of the violence;

4. appeal to all religious communities and ethnic and national groups to respect the right to freedom of religion, to seek reconciliation, and to engage in mutual forgiveness and healing;

5. awaken in all individuals and communities a sense of shared responsibility for the well-being of the human family as a whole and a recognition that all human beings regardless of religion, race, gender and ethnic origin have the right to education, health-care, and an opportunity to achieve a secure and sustainable livelihood;

6. Promote the equitable distribution of wealth within nations and among nations, eradicating poverty and reversing the current trend toward a widening gap between rich and poor;

7. Educate our communities about the urgent need to care for the earth's ecological systems and all forms of life and to support efforts to make environmental

protection and restoration integral to all development planning and activity;

8. Develop and promote a global reforestation campaign as a concrete and practical means for environmental restoration, calling upon others to join us in regional tree planting programs;
9. Join with the United Nations in the call for all nation states to work for the universal abolition of nuclear weapons and other weapons of mass destruction for the safety and security of life on this planet;
10. Combat those commercial practices and applications of technology that degrade the environment and the quality of human life; and
11. Practice and promote in our communities the values of the inner dimension of peace, including especially study, prayer, meditation, a sense of the sacred, humility, love, compassion, tolerance and a spirit of service, which are fundamental to the creation of a peaceful society.

We, as religious and spiritual leaders, pledge our commitment to work together to promote the inner and outer conditions that foster peace and the non-violent management and resolution of conflict. We appeal to the followers of all religious traditions and to the human community as a whole to cooperate in building peaceful societies, to seek mutual understanding through dialogue where there are differences, to refrain from violence, to practice compassion, and to uphold the dignity of all life.

In India, Hindus and Muslims have been living together, sharing centuries of common history and speaking Indian languages but dogmatism and politics keep them pitting against one another and sometimes religious leaders, particularly orthodox ones, add fuel to the fire, though it is their sacred duty to unite the people and not to divide them. These people want to tie their people to their doctrine in such a way that they start hating other religions and sometimes they become quite rigid and aggressive and their only agenda is to bring disgrace to the people professing other religions. It is quite rational that one professing a particular religion considers that religion to be the best. Once two of my students in Amity Institute of Advanced Legal Studies representing two different religions were arguing with raised pitch of voice that their respective religions were the best and none of them was ready to relent. One of the students professing the religion I follow solicited my intervention. I solved the problem in one sentence by asking 'A' to repeat after me the words. 'My religion is one of the best.' I also asked B to repeat the same words. I appreciated their smiling faces. This should be the approach of our religious and spiritual leaders. No religion teaches 'divide the people and enjoy'. Situation takes an ugly turn and the things become dangerous when one faith tries to win over the other. Once religious feelings are hurt, one becomes aggressive. There are such radicals in all communities. They are to be handled with care so that they may not trigger the violence at their sweet will to make things sore. Inter-faith dialogues must not be politically oriented and their focus must exclusively on values like human dignity, justice, charity, peace, support for the poor and the integrity of the nation. They (the preachers or religious persons) should tell and make it clear in their discourses that, ultimately, we are all praying to the same God. Respect for the prayers of another faith is, undoubtedly, an authentic form of dialogue but prayer should be held in such a way that ailing persons, in particular, and common men, in general, do not get disturbed. Any prayer with an intention to cause nuisance to one and all is not a prayer within the dictates of all religions. Use of loud speakers with a view to disturb the neighbours, blocking the traffic on roads deliberately, playing music before the mosques, etc., with a malafide intention of disturbing those offering prayers are the acts worth condemning. Praying is a peaceful activity with no aggressive overtones. Spirituality is the platform where all religions meet to unite and not to fight.

Separation of Religion and Politics

Religious codes should not be used for propagating and inculcating divisive feelings among the followers of different religions. Separation of politics from religion has been a debatable issue for years together and demand has been raised by certain quarters to bring legislation on the subject as also for seeking ban on foreign fund collection by communal and religious organisations and declaring religion as a private affair. Religion should not be used as a tool for creating animosity between Muslims and Hindus as it has already resulted in the loss of life and property to both the communities. But those who are not in favour of separation of religion from politics argue that there is no harm in making use of religion for positive reasons. They also quote the example of Mahatma Gandhi who led India to win independence from the British rule through a struggle that was founded on religious beliefs. Those were the days when religion was exclusively used for a cause so dear to every Indian, that is, for freedom movement and not for any personal motive. Leaders like Gandhi and

Maulana Azad had no personal agenda. They did not leave behind any estate. But in a religious society like ours complete divorce between religion and politics does not appear to be feasible. It can, however, be regulated by law. If religion has the overriding effect, then the words of Robert A. Heinlein, an American writer, will emerge in its practical form. To quote:

> "Almost any sect, cult, or religion will legislate its creed into law if it acquires the political power to do so."

How dismal it is to see the present-day India still in the grip of orthodoxy! Where is the spirit of scientific temperament, as envisaged in our Constitution? Freedom prospers only when religion is vibrant and interpreted only by those scholars who are competent to do so. It is something strange in our social and political life that every abject nonsense utterance is generally excused if the utterer can claim the sanction of religion. What type of pluralism it is! As a matter of fact, every religion is vibrant, if assessed objectively, and every Tom, Dick and Harry is not permitted to interpret religious scriptures subjectively or in the manner one likes.

8

Role of Youth and Intellectuals in Communal Harmony

Intellectuals and youth have a vital role to play in spreading the message of communal harmony to all corners of the country right from Jammu and Kashmir, famous and for its natural beauty and the highest and most beautiful mountain peaks, forests and meadows, massive glaciers, sparkling rivers, blue lakes, cherry blossoms and saffron fields, described as paradise on earth, to Kanniyakumari or Cape Comorin located on the southern-most tip of India where the Indian Ocean, the Bay of Bengal and the Arabian Sea meet.

In other words, this message must reach every home of India covering whole of Indian territory beginning from Himalayas in the north and passing through Indo-Gangetic plain and then crossing over the Vindhyachal mountains to enter the Deccan Peninsula and finally reaching southern-most tip. But it must be remembered that effective preaching is one which is preceded by practice. Mere giving sermons will not do. Charity begins from home. Thus, the lesson of communal harmony and national integration must be taught firstly at home and then at school. If the mind of the child is polluted at the initial stage, it becomes very difficult to change his/her mind-set. Sometimes, one may not get an opportunity to change it throughout one's life because stereo-types shall always hound him/her. Unfortunately, our educational system has become commercialised and our schools have become commercial hubs, of course not all. Some schools are imparting value-based education to all segments of the society and the most admirable feature of our education system is that our schools, even those run by religious organisations, do not discriminate on any ground whatsoever. Stray cases, being mere exceptions, cannot be the rule. This is the reason that Hindu and Muslim students have achieved great distinctions both in majority and minority run institutions. Communalism has always taken a back seat in our educational institutions and students have received full affection from their teachers, irrespective of their religious or ethical affiliations.

For a layman, persons having philosophical ideas, deeply involved in books, possessing various degrees, writers, professors, lawyers, doctors, engineers, scientists, artists, etc. may be intellectuals but it may not serve our purpose. In this context, we will have to set the parameters of being an intellectual which may be quite different from the perception of the common men, including our so-called educated class. For our purpose, an intellectual is one who can understand the merits of communal harmony and national integration and demerits of communal disharmony and disseminate this information to the people with the help of his intellectual capacity, knowledge, thoughts, intellect or understanding and mental powers or faculties. Any person, howmuchsoever qualified he/she may be, who divides the people is not an intellectual within the criteria set by us. A person who has no respect for humanity and human beings can never be an intellectual; he is worse than an illiterate person with love for his neighbours and countrymen. Likewise, intellectuals turned politicians who are more rooted in winning elections and have scant regard for human values and instead of playing larger role of unifying people and creating communal harmony, divide the people on one ground or the other cease to be intellectuals, no matter what tall claims do they make. However, if they continue to be honest and do not indulge in dirty politics, they deserve laurels and appreciation of the highest order. Such honest persons, may be in minority, have always been playing a positive role in political circles. Had they not been there, our political system would have collapsed by now.

The British believed that the communal hatred between Hindus and Muslims was the offshoot of false religious notions. They attributed it to the communal approach of Hindu and Muslim religious leaders who never missed a chance of arousing communal feelings of their respective communities even on petty traditional issues as discussed in previous chapters. Our intellectuals, too, inherited this theological approach from their colonial masters and continued to believe that communal violence was an inherent characteristic of the Indian society. Our intellectuals had, of late, realised that it was the 'divide and rule' policy of the British that resulted in communal violence. But the moot question is as to why this tragic situation continues even in independent secular India. How long we will continue to repeat this old story and blame the British for our own follies too?

The resolution of intra-community conflict has taken on a more complicated and certainly more challenging turn. During the pre-partition days, it used to be a routine between two communities rather amongst few of those communities or between two groups but now these violent conflicts appear to stem from demands by various communities living within states for the recognition of their specific identities, be religious or linguistic. Sometimes, we can also smell some foul play by outside agencies and anti-national elements within the country and sometimes politicians with vested interests also intervene pretending as if they were championing the cause of the aspirations of different groups of peoples just to get political mileage. It is also an established fact that it is also used as a political strategy by groups out and out to establish their separate identities even at the cost of national identity. It is a very dangerous situation because such groups do not hesitate even in indulging violence and challenging the authority of the State. Such groups do not hesitate even in indulging in terrorist activities. Thus, the state and intellectuals should make concerted efforts, adopt a pragmatic approach and evolve proper strategy to deal with the issue as under:

1. Sincere efforts must be made to know the root-causes of the communal violence in an objective and scientific manner.

2. Keeping in view the aspirations of different communities as also the collective national vision, such a harmonious system should be developed in which each community could maintain its separate identity and live freely and in dignity within its own separate identity thereby strengthening our composite

culture and building a strong, stable and united India—a vibrant pluralist, multi-religious and multi-cultural State-based on the values so cherished in the Indian Constitution thereby maintaining a balance between diversities in all the communities of the country and giving full respect to their political, social, cultural, religious and economic aspirations so that they may feel that all the communities are really at par for all purposes and none of them may suffer from any inferiority complex.

3. It is the duty of the State and the teachers to ensure that every child is imparted such education with the help of which he/she can attain the highest standards of intellectual honesty commensurating his/her age, stage of development and level of education and he/she gets an opportunity to socialise and mix freely with other children, irrespective of their caste, religion and the social status of their parents.

4. Religious education should preferably be imparted at home. If the law of the land permits imparting of such education in schools, it should be imparted in such a way that the recipient does not develop bias against any religion. It is not the business of the state to interfere in religious matters, but it has every right to regulate the education system to ensure fair treatment to all religious/other communities and objective outlook of the teachers and non-interference in their religious affiliations or lifestyle choices, such as dress code or food habits but this freedom must not be an intrusion in the religious freedom of other children. A healthy balance must be maintained between the two so that healthy atmosphere is available to the teacher and the taught. Fanaticism must give way to rationalism.

5. The intellectuals and liberal religious personalities must select best things of each religion and recommend to the government to include them in the school curriculum, so that the mind of our child student does not get polluted at the initial stage and he or she comes up with a feeling that all religions are good and there is no reason for hating anyone on the ground of religion or belief.

As quoted earlier, Dr. S. Radhakrishnan also believed that religion is a dynamic process, a renewed effort of the creative impulses working through exceptional individuals and seeking to uplift humankind to a new level. But unfortunately what we are noticing today is that we are not uplifting the humankind but we are bringing the humankind to the lowest level by misusing the religion and doing what every religion prohibits to do. In the changed socio-political scenario, the intellectuals have also lost their voice. It is high time that the intellectuals of our country must come forward to undertake the responsibility of creating congenial atmosphere in the country in which all of us may live in peace as brothers and sisters as was expected by the founding fathers of our Constitution. Justice Mr. Markandey Katju, former Judge, Supreme Court of India, presently Chairperson, Press Council of India, while delivering a lecture at Jamia Millia Islamia on 8.2.2011, had also said that intellectuals are the eyes of the society, and without intellectuals a society is blind... and a heavy responsibility lies on the intellectuals to advance forward.

Let the intellectuals tell the masses that Hindus and Muslims have to live and co-exist in India even if some of them hate some of them or all of them hate some of them or some of them hate all of them or some of them love them as individuals and not as a community or some of them remain indifferent. Some of us have to take the initiative. We can't build Rome in a day; we can't reunite the broken hearts in a jiffy. We cannot heal centuries-old wounds in days and months; we have miles to go; we cannot turn devils into saints overnight, and we cannot expect the victims of violence and injustice to forget everything so soon. But we have to give a wake-up call for mental transformation.

9

Indian Culture: Unity in Diversity

Religious profile of the populace is an important socio-cultural and demographic feature of a country's population. India's demographic and socio-economic character, too, is indicative of its complex and diverse civilisation. Its constitutional Sanskrit name '*Bharata*' has its own history. It is derived from the ancient Indian texts and it refers to the land that comprises India as *Bhârata,* the home of several religions. Hindus, Muslims, Christians, Sikhs, Zoroastrians (Parsis), Buddhists, Jains, Jews, Jevovah's witnesses, Bahaiis, etc., live in it as one people, the people of India. Although many people, especially in the western world, associate Islam with countries in the Middle East or North Africa though nearly two-thirds (62 per cent) of Muslims live in the Asia-Pacific region. It is a statistical reality that 344 million Muslims live in India and Pakistan, whereas total Muslim population in the entire Middle East-North Africa region is 317 million, as per Pew Research Center's report of 2012, titled 'Regional Distribution of Muslim Population by Region of 2010'. The country with the largest Muslim

Unity in Diversity : Yousuf Pathan (Muslim), Virat Kohli (Hindu), and Harbhajan Singh (Sikh)

population is Indonesia, where 87.2 per cent of the population identifies as Muslim. India has the world's second-largest Muslim population, though Muslims make up just 13.4 per cent of India's total population. India is a country filled with social and cultural markers. These markers define and classify its population into sub-populations based on religion, language, groups, castes, tribes, etc. These markers of social identity put it into the category of those civilisations who consider the concept of 'unity in diversity' as a practical proposition and not a mere slogan. **WE INDIANS ARE ONE AT THE PLAYGROUND AND THE BATTLEFIELD.**

Just see a Muslim (Yusuf Pathan), a Hindu (Virat Kohli) and a Sikh (Harbhajan Singh) carry the world's greatest batsman (Sachin Tendulkar), on their shoulders after winning the World Cup:

OUR HEROES: They laid down their lives for India.

Joginder Singh Indo-China '62 War

Abdul Hamid Indo-Pak '65 War

Albert Ekka 1971 B'desh War

Vikram Batra 1999 Kargil War

These heroes were awarded India's highest military honour, the Param Vir Chakra, posthumously.

Courtesy:allindianmuslims.com

Also see our war heroes professing different religions:

Courtesy:allindianmuslims.com

Indian Muslim soldiers praying during Kargil War' 99.

As regards Muslim population, it is growing at the pace slightly more than other communities if the figures are objectively analysed. The reason is that their migration to neighbouring countries has completely stopped and they are coming up, may not be at the desired pace, in all sectors, that is education, work participation, etc. They are gradually learning to co-exist with their Hindu brothers in a better way. Even media and newspapers are giving more coverage to them. Barring a microscopic minority who does not like them under any situation whatsoever or even under compulsion, majority of the majority community has reconciled to the changed situation. Now it is the duty of the Muslims to conduct in such a way that they (those who dislike them) are also won over sooner or later. They should not go off the track even if hardliners in their community ask them to pay those who hate them in the same coin. Both the communities have to live together in this country till the doomsday. They may, though they should not, pick up quarrel on petty issues. But they should always keep in mind that one quarrels only with one for whom he or she has some affection. For example, many of us pick up quarrel with our wives on petty issues like bad taste of food, unnecessary interference of their parents in their personal life or their frequent visits, but once the wife dies the same person sheds tears constantly because no one can be her substitute, even most obedient children and daughter-in-law or anyone else. It is an irrefutable fact. Thus, there is inseparable and indivisible relationship between Hindus and Muslims and it is to continue and flourish in the time to come. Even otherwise time is a great healing factor.

There is no area of operation or sector in the country or any walk of life in which persons professing different religions, speaking different languages and representing different groups of people are not represented. In India, there is a wide network of Muslim population spread over all parts of the country, though they make up just 13.4 per cent of India's total population.

Distribution of Population by Religious Groups and their Sex Ratios

Of the total population of India in 2001, 80.5 per cent are Hindus while Muslims account for 13.4 per cent and Christians 2.3 per cent respectively of the total population. In absolute numbers, proximately 828 million are Hindus, while Muslims are around 138 million out of India's total population of approximately 1,029 million. Sikhs account for 1.9 per cent of the total population. The proportion of Buddhists, Jains and other religions are 0.8 per cent, 0.4 per cent and 0.6 per cent, respectively. Sex ratio, which is the number of females per one thousand males, is 933 for all the religious groups at the national level. Hindus and Sikhs are below the national average, while the rest are above the average. The highest sex ratio is seen among Christians with 1009 females, while the lowest is among Sikhs (893). Constituting the largest segment of the population, the Hindus have a sex ratio of

Muslim Population in Indian States*

State	*Population*	*Muslims*	*Percentage of Muslims*
India	1,028,610,328	138,188,240	13.43
Andaman and Nicobar Islands	356,152	29,265	8.22
Andhra Pradesh	76,210,007	6,986,856	9.17
Arunachal Pradesh	1,097,968	20,675	1.88
Assam	26,655,528	8,240,611	30.92
Bihar	82,998,509	13,722,048	16.53
Chandigarh	900,635	35,548	3.95
Chhattisgarh	20,833,803	409,615	1.97
Dadra and Nagar Haveli	220,490	6,524	2.96
Daman and Diu	158,204	12,281	7.76
Delhi	13,850,507	1,623,520	11.72
Goa	1,347,668	92,210	6.84

(Contd.)

(Contd. Table)

State	*Population*	*Muslims*	*Percentage of Muslims*
Gujarat	50,671,017	4,592,854	9.06
Haryana	21,144,564	1,222,916	5.78
Himachal Pradesh	6,077,900	119,512	1.97
Jammu & Kashmir	10,143,700	6,793,240	66.97
Jharkhand	26,945,829	3,731,308	13.85
Karnataka	52,850,562	6,463,127	12.23
Kerala	31,841,374	7,863,842	24.70
Lakshadweep	60,650	57,903	95.47
Madhya Pradesh	60,348,023	3,841,449	6.37
Maharashtra	96,878,627	10,270,485	10.60
Manipur (Excl. 3 Sub-divisions)	2,166,788	190,939	8.81
Meghalaya	2,318,822	99,169	4.28

(Contd.)

(Contd. Table)

State	*Population*	*Muslims*	*Percentage of Muslims*
Mizoram	888,573	10,099	1.14
Nagaland	1,990,036	35,005	1.76
Orissa	36,804,660	761,985	2.07
Pondicherry	974,345	59,358	6.09
Punjab	24,358,999	382,045	1.57
Rajasthan	56,507,188	4,788,227	8.47
Sikkim	540,851	7,693	1.42
Tamil Nadu	62,405,679	3,470,647	5.56
Tripura	3,199,203	254,442	7.95
Uttar Pradesh	166,197,921	30,740,158	18.50
Uttaranchal	8,489,349	1,012,141	11.92
West Bengal	80,176,197	20,240,543	25.25

*Census 2001 (subject to change on 2011 Census religion-based data being available).

931, while Muslims, the second largest religious community, have 936.

Literacy Rate by Religion

The rate of literacy of the population computed for 2001 Census after excluding the population less than seven years of age is found to be 64.8 per cent for the whole country, male literacy percentage being 75.3, while the percentage for female being 53.7. Except Muslims and other religions, the rest of the major religions have literacy rates higher than the national average. Jains have the highest total literacy rate of 94.1 per cent, followed by Christians with 80.3 per cent. Buddhists with 72.7 per cent occupy the third position. The lowest total literacy rate of 47 per cent is found among other religions. Hindus have a total literacy rate of 65.1 per cent which is slightly above the national average, while Muslims have a total literacy rate of 59.1 per cent, below the national average.

Work Participation by Religion

Work participation rate, i.e., the percentage of workers to total population, for the country is 39.1 per cent. Religious groups which have work participation rate above the national average in descending order are other religions (48.4 per cent), Buddhists (40.6 per cent), Hindus (40.4 per cent) and Christians (39.7 per cent). Muslims have the lowest participation rate of 31.3 per cent, followed by Jains with 32.9 per cent and Sikhs with 37.7 per cent. Workers are broadly divided as cultivators, agricultural labourers, household industry workers and other workers. Other workers include workers in service, manufacturing, trade and commerce and allied activities. As much as 49.9 per cent of the total workers among other religions are cultivators which is much higher than the all-India rate of 31.7 per cent. Next highest is among Hindus with 33.1 per cent of the total workers. Sikhs with 32.4 per cent is also above the national average of 31.7 per cent. Among Jains, cultivators account for only 11.7 per cent which is very much below the national average. Agricultural labourers constitute 26.5 per cent of the total workers at the national level. The percentage is highest among Buddhists (37.6 per cent), other religions with 32.6 per cent comes in the second highest position. The percentage of agricultural labourers among Jains is as low as 3.3 per cent. In fact, only 15 per cent of the total workers among Jains work as cultivators and agricultural labourers. In household industry, the participation of workers among Muslims, which is 8.1 per cent, is almost double that of the national average of 4.2 per cent.

The above mentioned data explicitly reveal that Muslim presence is there in all sectors and walks of life. Here we are not analysing their socio-economic status. Our purpose is just to show that they are moving with the majority community in all walks of life, of course, with some variation in the acceleration of their pace.

Unity in diversity is the basic feature of the Indian Constitution and it has always been the guiding factor for the law-makers right from day one of the enforcement of the Constitution. Even the European Union adopted it as its motto only in 2000. Other countries had also followed suit. In United States, even Houses of Blues (the performance venues) have an emblem at the top of the stage with several religious symbols, and the phrase "Unity in Diversity." The concept of 'Unity in Diversity' is so popular that its equivalents are available in all major languages of the world but conceptual strength of 'Unity in Diversity' gets its real strength only when it is put into practice, particularly in religious matters. In

1938, in his book, *The World Order of Baha'ullah,* Shoghi Effendit, the Guardian of the Baha'i faith, had rightly said that **"unity in diversity" was the "watchword" for the "religion."** Any good statement from any quarter must be welcomed and judged on its merits. We should put in best efforts to have religious harmony in the true sense of the term and refrain from defaming any religion in any form which even otherwise is not legally permissible in our country. We should maintain a rational balance between secularism and the respect of freedom of religion. All of us know that growing anti-religious culture (particularly against certain religions) and discrimination against the persons professing different religions or faith deserve immediate attention and remedial measures. Hence, the governments should pay particular attention to this issue and take follow-up action to protect the places of worship and culture of all religions.

The historical saying that 'All Roads Lead to Rome' also means that different paths can lead to the same goal. Hence, all religions, too, lead to the same destination. Gandhi Ji also upholds different religions like different roads coming to the same point. Like differently shaped and sized five fingers of our hand, we may also agree to differ in regarding any particular issue because views may be conflicting and contradictory or the approach may also be somewhat different but this act of difference should be taken as another way of looking at the same point of view. This is the only way to attain the desired unity in diversity. Michael Novak, an American Catholic philosopher, theologist, journalist, novelist, and diplomat, has rightly said that unity in diversity is the highest possible attainment of a civilisation, a testimony to the noblest possibilities of the human race. This attainment is made possible through passionate concern for choice, in an atmosphere of social trust. This is also in the true spirit of the great tradition of *'Sarva dharma sambhava'* i.e., all religions are harmonious with each other and lead to God and thus one can follow the path he or she chooses. Tolerance and harmony is a weave through Indian philosophy, culture and society since ages. Gandhi Ji never subscribed to the view that there can or will be just one religion on the earth. He firmly believed in and preached for "*Sarva Dharma Sambhava* (Equal Approach to All Religions). His approach was very near to Swami Vivekanand's 'Universal Religion' or Tagore's 'Religion of Man'.

10

Can Better Indo-Pak Relations Help in Hindu-Muslim Unity?

The proposed heading may appear to be strange or non-patriotic to patriotic eyes and rightly so because internal relationship between different communities in a country is an internal matter of that country and another country or nation has nothing to do with it. But Indo-Pak relations are of special significance and have, undoubtedly, a bearing on such relationship for good and bad reasons. Since independence in 1947, India and Pakistan have followed a path of mutual animosity, mistrust and hatred and both of them have been blaming each other. There is no room for feeling of solid dislike by either of the nations as far as the diplomatic relationship is concerned. It takes the nations nowhere and results in unwarranted armed conflicts, wars and day-to-day skirmishes on one pretext or the other thereby affecting the polity and the people adversely from all points of view that is politically, socially, economically as also culturally.

Pakistan, being carved out of India, in 1947 became a theocratic state based on Mohd. Ali Jinnah's two-nation theory and India chose to be a secular state and it became home of a nation comprising 85 per cent Hindus, the majority community, and rest being religious and linguistic minorities, that is, then more than 10 per cent Muslims as also good number of Sikhs, Christians and other microscopic minorities professing different religions and speaking different languages. It was, undoubtedly, a geographical disaster for India and a physical disaster for Indian Muslims, being the worst victims of partition. What people of Pakistan feel about it, it is for them to opine whether they are the gainers or losers. No one has a right to put words into their mouth. They are an independent nation and they have their own credibility. To what extent and how do they maintain their credibility depends on positive thinking of Pak government and the people of Pakistan as also the agenda of those out and out to sabotage the cause. Soon after the partition, about 17 million people were forced to flee from their homes and travel to either Pakistan or India, as the case may be. It is described as the largest exchange of populations in the world history, but the ground situation clearly reveals that it was not an exchange; it was a carnage, Muslims on the one side and Sikhs and Hindus on the other. Exchange is a peaceful process in which something is given in return for something received or parted with. Had it been so, resulting bloodshed in Punjab and West Bengal regions would not have left more than one million people dead and wounded. Had both the governments shown the same seriousness in peaceful exchange of population that they had displayed in the division of their assets, weapons, money, archaeological treasures, etc., the holocaust could be avoided and millions of hearts would not have broken and communal harmony so jolted.

The people in Pakistan were our people before 1947 and we loved them as our brothers and sisters and have also been the co-sharers of the same heritage, though some of the hardliners on both sides of the border may not accept this self-speaking historical fact. But today, because of a line having drawn across the nation by the British, they are no longer our brothers and sisters, if their nationalities be the only criterion to judge this relationship. Fact of the matter is that cultural relationship never comes to an end. We believe that the partition of India was the death of India's composite culture but, at the same time, we cannot rule out its resurrection or its inherent existence. In a rapidly changing world people on both sides of the border would like to see greater mobility of people and better cultural relations to get rid of the vicious circle within which they feel suffocated. The situation warrants that the poison that currently informs the politics on both sides must be cut down or be converted into an ineffective substance. In such a situation no advocate of better cultural relations between these two countries can be subjectively described as pro-India or pro-Pakistan. Neighbourhood is also a bond of real brotherhood if discharged or acted upon in true spirit and not as *aasteen ka saanp* (snake in the sleeve or a hidden enemy). Scores cannot be settled by killing innocent people or innocent soldiers guarding the Indo-Pak border or resorting to aggressive misadventures including terrorism.

As already stated, WE CANNOT CHANGE THE NEIGHBOURS, BUT WE CAN CHANGE THEIR HEARTS AND MIND-SET. The relationship between these two countries has faced various ups and downs and passed through various phases during the last more than six decades after India's independence, but it continued to deteriorate after successive events like Mumbai attack by terrorists, attack on Indian Parliament,

Samjhota Express bombing, beheading of an Indian soldier, fatal attack on Sarabjit Singh, the Indian prisoner held in Pakistani jail, and attack on Pakistani prisoner in Jammu Jail. Probably their relationship did not suffer as badly even after different wars and armed conflicts between India and Pakistan as it did in recent years. It will not be out of place to refer to the past history of relations between India and Pakistan in brief so that remedial measures may be suggested. There have been various disputes, wars and other problems between these two countries right from day one, such as Kashmir conflict, insurgency in Kashmir, war of 1965, Bangladesh Liberation War of 1971, Bengal refugees issue, Indian and Pakistani nuclear tests, Kargil War, Siachin conflict, other territorial disputes, water disputes, etc. There have been numerous attempts to improve the relationship and various agreements made and confidence-building measures taken from time to time between these two countries, such as Tashkent Agreement, Shimla Agreement, Agra Summit, Lahore Summit, Delhi-Lahore and Kashmir bus service, but certain unfortunate incidents, a few mentioned above, spoil the whole show and everything is back to square one, sooner or later. At one stage, cricket diplomacy was also used as a tool for improving Indo-Pak ties.

'The first test series was played in 1951-52 when Pakistani team went to India and in 1954-55 Indian team came to Pakistan to play cricket. But from 1962-77, no match was played on the home grounds of both India and Pakistan due to 1965 and 1971 Wars between the two countries... The higher political leadership also goes to stadiums if both countries are playing with each other and buck up their respective teams. There are special messages on TV news if one country beats the other by the political leadership. The former President of Pakistan, Zia-ul-Haq, went to India in 1987 to watch a match between two countries on invitation of Indian Prime Minister Rajiv Gandhi...Today cricket is considered as a part of riot, uprising and rivalry between the masses of the both countries, as the players of both countries were taken as fighting for the win of their country and defeating the rivals. People celebrate the victory on roads and streets if they win the other in cricket (Holm, A.N. and Holm, A.N. (2008). *Batting for Peace.* Germany: VDM Publishers).

LET GONE BE BYGONE. WE CAN START AFRESH. WHY PEACE AND RECONCILIATION BE NOT GIVEN A CHANCE? HAS ANY WAR OR ACT OF VIOLENCE, AGRESSION, EXTREMISM OR TERRORISM SOLVED ANY PROBLEM PERMANENTLY IN ANY PART OF THE WORLD? CAN ANY ONE LAY ONE'S HANDS ON ANY SUCH STORY?

Both India and Pakistan can engage in proxy war and other aggressive ventures to destabilise each other but the moot question, whether it will be a viable proposition to bring an end to terror and other aggressive provocations, shall remain unanswered and if it is answered the answer would be that unstable India and unstable Pakistan shall not be beneficial to both the countries; some third party may take advantage of this cat and monkey story. Violence results in loss of life and property and brings sighs for one and all, the losers as also the winners! One can get rid of divisions and differences of the past through peace, aspiration for unity and, above all, through positive approach even at the cost of betrayal from the other side. Those with feeble understanding and perpetuating malice towards others take more time in accepting ground realities. If East Germany and West Germany can put their past behind them and aspire for a common future, why can't Indians and Pakistanis? Undoubtedly, it is an uphill task but if nothing is impossible in war; nothing is impossible in peace, too. Blood does not ooze from the wounds constantly. It ultimately stops either through proper treatment or through healing with the passage of time.

Instead of repenting on past follies or repeating the history of efforts having made and confidence-building measures taken from time to time during all regimes to sort out differences between these two divided nations, we should impress upon Nawaz Sharif that peace (though beneficial to both the nations) is more important to Pakistan because internal problems of Pakistan require immediate attention and cannot allow him to take up any aggressive strategic ventures and play with the fire. His constraints like Army and ISI and fanatic groups have also started realising that peace must be given a chance. Moreover, the world scenario has made them wise enough to think rationally. Barring a few fanatics of extreme degree who even do not know that there are certain norms even in madness, they (may not be in sufficient number) also want peace and better relationship with India happily or otherwise as a compulsive measure. Some reports suggest positive change in their mindset. In this situation, Nawaz Sharif's offer for better relationship with India, may be formal one, is laudable and should be welcomed and positive efforts be made to bring him to the negotiating table because no one can live in peace if his/her relations with his or her neighbour are strained. We both the nations should join hands in *jihad (crusade)* against eradication of illiteracy and removal of poverty and other evils like corruption, sexual crimes, gender

Social Indicators for India and Pakistan According to UNDP's Human Development Report, 2011

	India	*Pakistan*
Human Development Index ranking out of total 187 countries of the world (from high to low).	134	145
HDI Value	0.547	0.504
Life expectancy at birth	65.4	65.4
Mean years of Schooling (years)	4.4	4.9
Expected years of schooling	10.3	6.9
Gross National Income	3468	2550
Gender Inequality Index		
Rank	129	115
Value	0.617	0.573

(Contd.)

(Contd. Table)

	India	*Pakistan*
Maternal mortality ratio	230	260
Seats in National Parliament (per cent female)	10.7	21
Population with at least secondary education (percentages 25 and older)		
Female	26.6	23.5
Male	50.4	46.8
Adult Literacy rate (percentages 15 and older)	62.8	55.5
Mortality		
under 5 per 1000 live births	28	87
adult per 1000 people	111	189
Health adjusted life expectancy	61	55
Total expenditure on Health (percentage of GDP)	4.2	2.6

discrimination, malnutrition, etc. We must not feel happy if by sheer chance one is above or below the other in the serial wise global list of these evils. Our concern must be to see as to why our name appears in the list of erring nations. We must strive hard for better economic, cultural and diplomatic relations with each other and try to improve their social and economic status. Let them try to improve their present status as recorded in the table below based on authentic source of information.

It is common knowledge that the whole world has already suffered a lot at the hands of violent groups with different nomenclatures and even the 'creators' and 'promoters' of these groups have faced and are still facing their fury. (The author, being a human rights writer, is avoiding to mention the names of these groups so that the readers may not feel that he is prejudiced and any subjective approach to the problem may have a negative impact on peace process as these groups are also coming forward for peace and patch up with those with whom they have been crossing swords in different parts of the world at the national and international level). Intelligent readers can easily read between the lines. Disaster diplomacy, that is, help in tragedy builds bridges between nations and it should continue but there are hardly any examples of resolution of any serious conflicts with this tool, reason being that the memory of humanitarian assistance fades with the passage of time. Hence pragmatic, meaningful and sincere diplomatic efforts must continue.

Improving Indo-Pak Relations Through Trade

Both India and Pakistan are members of the South Asia Free Trade Area (SAFTA) established in January 2006, but the trade between them is no match to what it ought to have been though there is enough scope and there are ample opportunities for its expansion. Both of them have been making tall claims of giving the status of most favoured nation to each other but the volume of trade continues to remain almost static. Total trade (exports plus imports) between India and Pakistan in 2008 amounted to a little more than US$2 billion, up from a paltry US$500 million in 2000. The situation continues to be unsatisfactory and even now Pakistan accounts for less than 0.5 per cent of India's trade, and India accounts for a little over one per cent of Pakistan's trade. The situation was not so bad in early post-partition years though the bitter memories of partition were still hounding the people on both the sides. In 1948-49, 70 per cent of Pakistan's trading transactions were with India, while 63 per cent of Indian exports went to Pakistan. If figures of informal trade via third countries are taken into account, the total transactions amounted to US$2-3 billion per year and even the cost of trade was very low but these two countries did not learn any lesson from this healthy situation and continued to adhere to their stereo-type non-pragmatic emotional approach. Had both of them not been so rigid, they would have saved billions of dollars by now and sky would have been the limit for both the countries. They made certain desperate advances to solve political disputes, but no serious exercise was made to improve the trade relations.

Pakistan's list of items of goods covered under Most Favoured Nation (MFN) status for India continues to be very limited. Thus, India can export only these paltry items of goods. On the other hand, Pakistan complains of India's high tariff rates particularly for goods in which it may be interested, such as textiles, leather, mineral onyx, etc. Both the countries have not made any serious efforts to improve transport facilities, such as better railway, road and sea connections. It is really disheartening to note that there is hardly any trade in services or Foreign Direct Investment (FDI) between the two countries. But still they have the miles to move on. The road is not blocked. Some of Pakistani economists feel that growing trade with India, a country with much higher rate of growth as compared to Pakistan, shall ruin some of their industries as they will not be able to compete. But their economists must appreciate that if India shall have edge over them, they may also re-emerge by putting the Austrian theory of 'destructive capitalism' into practice according to which a country may suffer in the initial stage of capital reformation but with the growth of business circulation of capital increases and so its inflow and as a result of availability of more capital new sectors come up and they absorb those persons including professionals who had lost their jobs. Thus, the loss suffered because of closure of one sector opens new avenues for earning profit and providing more employment. Here is a practical example of Ecuador, a Latin American country, may be quoted. Sometime ago their industrial production and exports indicated the negative trends as a result of which their economy suffered a lot. But a petty idea having come into the mind of a businessman reversed the whole situation. This country is a big producer of flowers. After a market survey of United States, one of the biggest buyers of flowers, exporters of this country started to export their flowers to the US. Within a period of just two years, the export of this non-traditional item proved to be a boom in the revival of their economy. They earned billions of dollars during this period that helped this country to be a prosperous state. Things change with the passage of time. At one time, the US was the biggest manufacturer in the world and its manufacturing sector had a 75 per cent share in GDP, but now the share has gone down to 25 per cent. If India, being a more advanced country in almost all the sectors, is in a more advantageous position, Pakistan, too, is not at loss. They should also explore such opportunities in India. For example, their washing machines and electric fans manufactured at large scale in Gujarat (a town in Pakistan) may be the saleable items in India. They can supply motor car parts to India, one of the biggest manufacturers of cars. Their drug industry is in a bad shape. If India enters into this market there, they will be bound to improve the quality of their products which would be a healthy phenomenon. There will be many takers of their medicines.

Improving Cultural Ties

India and Pakistan are the co-sharers of common cultural heritage and social values. They were part of the same history till the partition of India in 1947. Social and cultural values may change, but the history remains intact. Both the countries suffered at the hands of invaders and colonial powers as a single entity, that is, India, for centuries together. Both of them suffered at their own hands, too, during the tragic communal holocaust of 1947.

After the Independence, both India and Pakistan fought three wars (1965, 1971 and 1999), indulged in various skirmishes and war of words, faced border tensions, terrorism, etc., but cultural ties, if not further strengthened, did not face any serious setback. Culture-based on almost same cultural and social values, same language, same weather, same geographical features, same festivities, same traditions, same food habits, same jokes (of course with minor variations), same dress code, same sources of entertainment cannot die in a few decades. Songs of Indian films can be heard in almost every household of Pakistan and even the shopping malls, public carriers, etc. Shah Rukh Khan, who is married to an Indian Hindu girl, is quite popular in Pakistan and so Salman Khan and Amir Khan as also our other actors and actresses. Shah Rukh Khan says:

"The language, the name of God, should not become an issue between couples, between neighbours, society and the whole of the country. I stand for the young, educated Indian and when I say Indian it could be Muslim, Hindu or Sikh." (Rao, S. (2010). *Shah Rukh Khan: Symbol of Indian Secularism.* Pakistan: South Asian Journal. (Journal # 29, named: Cinema in South Asia).

The posters of Indian actors and actresses can be seen anywhere in Pakistan. Indian serials portraying simple common life of the region are quite popular in Pakistan. Our singers like Lata Mangeshkar and Mohd. Rafi and Pakistani singers like Mehdi Hassan and Rahat Fateh Ali Khan have been the darling of both the nations.

But the situation is not so rosy in other sectors. Objectivity of material contained in the text books on both sides has always been an issue. The only difference is that authorities in India are more receptive in such matters and whenever such complaints are brought to their knowledge they act promptly.

Media plays a major role in uniting and dividing the people. Media should avoid a negative role in building relationships between the two nations or countries. David Binder of *New York Times* describes negative role of media as tyranny or cruelty of victimology. Indian and Pakistani media must refrain from playing such a negative role. Cricket diplomacy, as mentioned above, if taken in true spirit, is also a positive exercise for maintaining cultural amity between these two nations.

Sikh's pilgrimage to Pakistan and Pak Hindus' and Muslims' visits to their respective shrines in India must be encouraged. Civil society and peace activists and NGOs like *Aman Ki Asha* (Hope for Peace), a joint venture of two daily newspapers of India, South Asian Free Media Association (SAFMA), Pakistan and such other organisations and human rights activists must step-up their efforts to promote peace and harmony between the two nations.

Educational Cooperation

According to the UNDP's Human Development Report, 2011, India's adult literacy rate (percentages 15 and older) is 62.8 and Pakistan's 55.5. On the face of the record, the difference appears to be narrow one but no one can deny that India's educational system and institutions are much better than that of Pakistan. India is producing better stuff and providing human resource even to most developed countries of the world. However, Pakistani graph of education is also moving upward at an accelerated pace and their doctors, engineers and scientists are rendering valuable services in developed countries like United States of America and U.K. They are also maintaining good relations with their Indian colleagues there. So, there is ample scope of bilateral cooperation in academic field, too. Most of the Indian and Pakistani students go to the West for higher education, particularly for technical education and face acute financial and immigration problems, besides many other social problems. These bilateral ties may make the things easier and they may also not suffer from home sickness because of cultural similarity.

Exchange Programmes etc.

Cultural exchange programmes between artists, human rights activists, students, writers, scholars, parliamentarians, etc., of both the countries, particularly in the spirit of UN New Millennium Declaration and UN Global Agenda, may help in promoting peace and harmony between these two nations and easing the situation, particularly in difficult hours.

Tourism

Every Indian and Pakistani must be eligible to see historical buildings in both the countries. Nehru-Liaqat Pact may be reviewed and re-written after thorough deliberations between both the countries. Pakistanis should not be alien to the Taj Mahal, so Indians to Mohanje Daro and Harappa. Grant of visa must be a process without tears for all categories of visitors.

The following extract from UN Global Agenda for Dialogue among Civilisations suggesting measures to improve relations between different countries may be used as guiding principles for better Indo-Pak relations:

- Facilitating and encouraging interaction and exchange among all individuals, *inter alia*, intellectuals, thinkers and artists of various societies and civilisations;

- Promoting of mutual visits and meetings of experts in various fields from different civilisations, cultures and backgrounds, which provide an opportunity for discovering commonalities among various civilisations and cultures;

- Exchange of visits among representatives of the arts and culture and the organisation of cultural festivals through which people will have a chance of getting acquainted with other cultures;
- Sponsorship of conferences, symposiums and workshops to enhance mutual understanding, tolerance and dialogue among civilisations;
- Planning sports competitions, Olympiads and scientific competitions, with a view to encouraging positive interaction among youth from different backgrounds and cultures;
- Reinvigorating and encouraging translation and dissemination of basic manuscripts and books and studies representing different cultures and civilisations;
- Promotion of historical and cultural tourism;
- Incorporation of programmes to study various cultures and civilisations in educational curriculums, including the teaching of languages, history and socio-political thoughts of various civilisations, as well as the exchange of knowledge, information and scholarship among academia;
- Advancement of research and scholarship to achieve an objective understanding of the characteristics of each civilisation and the differences, as well as ways and means to enhance constructive interaction and understanding among them;
- Utilisation of communication technologies, including audio-video, printed press, multi-media and the internet, to disseminate the message of dialogue and

understanding throughout the globe and depict and publicise historical instances of constructive interaction among different civilisations;

- Provision of equitable opportunities for participation in the dissemination of all information, with a view to achieving an objective understanding of all civilisations and enhancing constructive interaction and cooperative engagement among civilisations;
- Implementation of programmes to enhance the spirit of dialogue, understanding and rejection of intolerance, violence and racism among people, particularly the youth;
- Utilising the existence of migrants in various societies in bridging the gap of understanding between cultures;
- Consultation to articulate effective mechanisms to protect the rights of all people to maintain their cultural identity, while facilitating their integration into their social environment.

It is not only the Global Agenda, even other UN documents like United Nations Millennium Declaration are also of special significance to both the countries. Instead of entering into war of words on various issues, they should collectively strive hard to implement some of the most important provisions of the declaration reproduced below:

" Heads of different States and Governments had *inter alia*, having gathered at United Nations Headquarters in New York from 6 to 8 September 2000, at the dawn of a new millennium, had *inter alia* considered certain fundamental values to be essential to international relations in the twenty-first century, a few mentioned below:

- **Equality:** No individual must be denied the opportunity to benefit from development. The equal rights and opportunities of women and men must be assured.
- **Solidarity:** Global challenges must be managed in a way that distributes the costs and burdens fairly in accordance with basic principles of equity and social justice. Those who suffer or who benefit least deserve help from those who benefit most.
- **Tolerance:** Human beings must respect one another, in all their diversity of belief, culture and language. Differences within and between societies should be neither feared nor repressed, but cherished as a precious asset of humanity.

These heads had also declared that they will-spare no effort to free our peoples from the scourge of war, whether within or between States, which has claimed more than five million lives in the past decade and eliminate the dangers posed by weapons of mass destruction.

- Strengthen respect for the rule of law in international as in national affairs.
- To take concerted action against international terrorism, and to accede as soon as possible to all the relevant international conventions.
- To redouble our efforts to implement our commitment to counter the world drug problem.

- To intensify our efforts to fight transnational crime in all its dimensions, including trafficking as well as smuggling in human beings and money laundering.

We will spare no effort to free our fellow men, women and children from the abject and dehumanising conditions of extreme poverty

We resolve therefore to create an environment – at the national and global levels alike – which is conducive to development and to the elimination of poverty.

- To halve, by the year 2015, the proportion of the world's people whose income is less than one dollar a day and the proportion of people who suffer from hunger and, by the same date, to halve the proportion of people who are unable to reach or to afford safe drinking water.
- To ensure that, by the same date, children everywhere, boys and girls alike, will be able to complete a full course of primary schooling and that girls and boys will have equal access to all levels of education.
- By the same date, to have reduced maternal mortality by three quarters, and under-five child mortality by two thirds, of their current rates.
- To have, by then, halted, and begun to reverse, the spread of HIV/AIDS, the scourge of malaria and other major diseases that afflict humanity.
- To provide special assistance to children orphaned by HIV/AIDS.
- By 2020, to have achieved a significant improvement in the lives of at least 100 million slum dwellers as proposed in the "Cities without Slums" initiative.

- To promote gender equality and the empowerment of women as effective ways to combat poverty, hunger and disease and to stimulate development that is truly sustainable.
- To develop and implement strategies that give young people everywhere a real chance to find decent and productive work.
- To encourage the pharmaceutical industry to make essential drugs more widely available and affordable by all who need them in developing countries.
- To develop strong partnerships with the private sector and with civil society organisations in pursuit of development and poverty eradication.
- To ensure that the benefits of new technologies, especially information and communication technologies are available to all.

We must spare no effort to free all of humanity, and above all, our children and grandchildren, from the threat of living on a planet irredeemably spoilt by human activities, and whose resources would no longer be sufficient for their needs.

- To intensify cooperation to reduce the number and effects of natural and manmade disasters."

Both the countries must try to ignore the follies of the past without going into the exercise of pinpointing the defaulter and try to translate the said agenda of the United Nations into practice to have a better India and better Pakistan. But it must be remembered that it cannot be done unilaterally; it should be a reciprocal exercise. 'Stabbing in the back' policy never succeeds.

11

Proposed Legislative Measures to Curb Communal Violence and Disharmony

Communal disharmony and the resultant communal violence have become a distinct feature of communalism in India and assumed the form of a multi-factorial disorder because many a factor are involved in causing such a sub-human rather inhuman phenomenon, though we the Indians are considered as one of the most tolerant nations in the world. These factors are divisive, mostly hidden and sometimes open, communal propaganda, communal instigation by individuals and so-called political leader (*as no sane and career conscious leaders will indulge in such dirty politics and will never allow his linen to be dirty*), indifferent attitude of law enforcement agencies, delayed justice and poor rate of conviction, more or less indifferent attitude of political parties towards this issue, breeding of wrong-doers in traditional orthodox communal families and societal atmosphere, misuse of religion, subjective interpretation of religious books and scriptures, ignoring message of love and brotherhood given by all religions, dissemination of unfounded information to arouse communal feelings, exclusivistic approach of the followers of different religions to prove superiority of their respective religions aggressively and not through rational preaching, societal compulsions and, above all, the age-old mind-set of all communities. No one can divide us the individuals or the nation as a whole if we have no inclination towards division and divisive forces. Let us try introspection.

Sometimes, when two groups, representing two different religions, indulge in a clash even in purely a private matter or dispute, defeat of one is taken as insult to the whole community and this simple feeling is enough to arouse communal passion of both the conflicting groups which on occasions takes the shape of a full-fledged communal riot; it is the off-shoot of age-old animosity between these two communities for no cogent reasons, as we have discussed in previous chapters. Both the communities have to come out of this vicious circle. There is a long history of communal violence in our country and besides providing complete protective cover to minorities in the constitution of India, several provisions have been incorporated in Indian Penal Code to ensure harmony between persons professing different religions, as discussed in Chapter 6, a few being reproduced below:

The Indian Penal Code, 1860 Section	*Description of Offence*
153B	Imputations, assertions prejudicial to national integration.
295	Injuring or defiling place of worship with the intent to insult the religion of any class.
295A	Deliberate and malicious acts intending to outrage religious feelings of any class by insulting its religion or religious beliefs.

296	Disturbing religious assembly.
Despite these legislative 297	Trespassing on burial places, etc.
298	Uttering words, etc., with deliberate intent to wound religious feelings of any person.

Despite these legislative measures, communal disharmony is a very serious problem confronting the state and the nation even today. A brief description of communal riots as recorded in the chronology of communal violence in India is the eye opener.

Major Pre-partition Riots

1893—Bombay Riot;

1926—Calcutta Riots,

Major Post-partition Riots after Bloodshed of 1947

1948—Noakhali Riots,

1969—Ahmedabad Riots,

1979—Aligarh and Jamshedpur Riots,

1980—Moradabad Riots,

1984—Delhi Sikh Riots,

1987—Meerut Riots,

1989—Bhagalpur Riots,

1992—Mumbai Riots,

2002—Gujarat Riots,

2013—Muzaffar Nagar Riots.

Besides the above-mentioned major communal riots, communal riots have also taken place in other parts of the country.

In this background, the Central Government has decided to tackle this menace and has brought a legislation in the form of Prevention of Communal and Targeted Violence (Access to Justice and Reparations) Bill, 2011 to respect, protect and fulfill the right to equality before law and equal protection of law by imposing duties on the Central Government and the State Governments, to exercise their powers in an impartial and non-discriminatory manner to prevent and control targeted violence, including mass violence, against Scheduled Castes, Scheduled Tribes and religious minorities in any state in the Union of India, and linguistic minorities in any state in the Union of India; to thereby uphold secular democracy; to help secure fair and equal access to justice and protection to these vulnerable groups through effective provisions for investigation, prosecution and trial of offences under the Act; to provide for restorative relief and reparation, including rehabilitation and compensation to all persons affected by communal and targeted violence; and for matters connected herewith and incidental thereto. It is never too late. Appreciation of a positive step should be preferred to condemnation of delay because delayed justice is, undoubtedly, a better situation if compared to the situation of complete absence of justice. Even the maxims like "justice delayed is justice denied" get changed with the passage of time.

This Act shall apply to the whole of India excluding the state of Jammu and Kashmir and shall come into force within one year from the date of its passage and any person liable under any Indian law including this Act, to be tried for an offence committed beyond India shall be dealt in accordance with the provisions of this Act for any act committed beyond India in the same manner as if such act had been committed within India.

Terms of Special Significance Defined in the Proposed Legislation

Its definition clause (Section 3) defines certain terms used in the Act some of which have become a debatable issue, particularly the definition of the term "Group".

Communal and Targeted Violence

It means and includes any act or series of acts, whether spontaneous or planned, resulting in injury or harm to the person and or property, knowingly directed against any person by virtue of his or her membership of any group.

Group

It means a religious or linguistic minority, in any state in the Union of India, or Scheduled Castes and Scheduled Tribes within the meaning of clauses (24) and (25) of Article 366 of the Constitution of India.

Hostile Environment against a Group

It means an intimidating or coercive environment that is created when a person belonging to any group as defined under this Act, by virtue of his or her membership of that group, is subjected to any of the following acts:

(i) boycott of the trade or businesses of such person or making it otherwise difficult for him or her to earn a living; or

(ii) publicly humiliate such person through exclusion from public services, including education, health and transportation or any act of indignity; or

(iii) deprive or threaten to deprive such person of his or her fundamental rights; or

(iv) force such person to leave his or her home or place of ordinary residence or livelihood without his or her express consent; or

(v) any other act, whether or not it amounts to an offence under this Act, that has the purpose or effect of creating an intimidating, hostile or offensive environment.

Internally Displaced Person

It means and includes any person, whether or not he or she belongs to a group as defined under this Act, who has been forced or obliged to leave his or her home or place of ordinary residence as a result of or in order to avoid the effects of organised communal or targeted violence to any other location within India. The term 'internal displacement' shall be construed accordingly;

Victim

It means any person belonging to a group as defined under this Act, who has suffered physical, mental, psychological or monetary harm or harm to his or her property as a result of the commission of any offence under this Act, and includes his or her relatives, legal guardian and legal heirs...

Offences and Punishments/Penalties under the Act

Offences

Sexual assault - A person is said to commit sexual assault if he or she commits any of the following acts against a person belonging to a group by virtue of that person's membership of a group:

(a) Against a woman:

(i) rape;

(ii) gang rape;

(iii) rape or gang rape as part of or in the course of organised communal and targeted violence.

(b) Against any person, without their consent or against their will,

(i) the introduction by a man of his penis or any other body part or an object into vagina, mouth or anus, to any extent;

(ii) causing harm or hurt to reproductive organs or genital organs;

(iii) exposing one's sexual organs in front of any person;

(iv) sexual contact of any sort, including the performance of sexual acts for any length of time;

(v) removing the person's clothes, partially or fully, or compelling that person to undress himself or herself, partially or fully, in public view or otherwise, or parading that person in undressed state in public view or otherwise;

(vi) any other act or conduct that subjects that person to sexual indignity.

Provided that where sexual assault under Sub-section (a) or (b) is committed as part of or in the course of organised communal and targeted violence, it shall not be necessary to prove that the said act was committed against the victim without their consent or against their will.

Explanation : For the purposes of this section, consent shall mean :

(a) Explanation 1 : The unequivocal voluntary agreement where the person has by words, gestures, or any form of non-verbal communication, communicated willingness to participate in the act referred to in this section; (b) "Unequivocal voluntary agreement" means willingness given for specific and be limited to the express act consented to under this section.

(b) Explanation 2 : For the purposes of this section, consent obtained by duress, threat, terror, fear, coercion, undue influence, misrepresentation or mistake of fact shall not be unequivocal voluntary agreement.

Hate Propaganda: Notwithstanding anything contained in any other law for the time being in force, whoever publishes, communicates or disseminates by words, either spoken or written, or by signs or by visible representation or by electronic or other means of mass communication or otherwise acts inciting hatred causing clear danger of violence against a group or persons belonging to that group, in general or specifically, or disseminates or broadcasts any information, or publishes or displays any advertisement or notice, that could reasonably be construed to demonstrate an intention to promote or incite hatred or expose or is likely to expose the group or persons belonging to that group to such hatred, is said to be guilty of hate propaganda...

Organised Communal and Targeted Violence: Whoever, being an individual, singly or jointly with others or being a part of an association or on behalf of an association or acting under the influence of an association, engages in continuing unlawful activity of a widespread or systematic nature knowingly directed against a group or part thereof, by virtue of their membership of that group, by use of violence or threat of violence or intimidation or coercion or by committing sexual assault or other unlawful means, is said to commit the offence of organised communal and targeted violence (Section 10)

Offence under the Indian Penal Code, 1860 - The offences under the Indian Penal Code, 1860 provided in:

(a) Schedule II, Part A of this Act; or

(b) Schedule II, Part B of this Act, when committed against any person belonging to a group by virtue of his or her membership to that group,

shall be deemed to be offences of communal and targeted violence under this Act and shall be dealt with accordingly. (Section 11)

Torture – Whoever, being a public servant, or under the control or direction of or with the acquiescence of a public servant, intentionally inflicts pain or suffering, whether mental or physical, or inflicts cruel, inhuman or degrading treatment, on a person belonging to a group by virtue of his or her membership of a group, including causing grievous hurt or danger to life, limb or health or sexual assault, for the purposes of obtaining from him or her or a third person information or a confession or punishing him or her for an act he or she or a third person committed or is suspected of having committed, or intimidating or coercing him or her or a third person or for any other purpose, is said to inflict torture.

Provided that nothing contained in this Section shall apply to any pain, hurt or danger as aforementioned caused or inflicted in accordance with law. (Section 12)

Dereliction of Duty - When any person who is or was a public servant not removable from his or her office save by or with the sanction of the Central Government or State Government, as the case may be, authorised to act under any provision of this Act:

(a) exercises the authority vested in him or her colourably or in a manner otherwise than provided under law for the time being in force, which causes or is likely to lead to an offence of communal and targeted violence or by which he or she intends to screen or knowing it to be likely that he or she will thereby screen any person from legal punishment; or

(b) omits to exercise lawful authority vested in him or her under law, without reasonable cause, thereby fails to prevent the commission of communal and targeted violence, breach of public order or disruption in the maintenance of services and supplies essential to a group, shall be guilty of dereliction of duty... (Secton 13)

Offences by public servants for breach of command responsibility - (1) Whoever, being a public servant in command, control or supervision of the armed forces or security forces as defined under clause (a) of Section 3 of this Act or assuming command whether lawfully or otherwise, fails to exercise control over persons under his or her command, control, or supervision and as a result of such failure offences under this Act are committed, by persons under his or her command, control or supervision, or as a result of such failure the said persons fail to discharge their duties under this Act or any other law for the time being in force, shall be guilty of the offence of breach of command responsibility...(Section 14)

Offences by other superiors for breach of command responsibility - (1) Whoever, being any non-state actor or superior or office-bearer of any association as defined under clause (b) of Section 3 of this Act and other than those mentioned under Section 14, in command, control or supervision of any association or assuming command vested in him or her or otherwise, fails to exercise control over subordinates under his or her command, control, supervision and as a result of such failure offences under this Act are committed by subordinates under his or her command, control or supervision, shall be guilty of offences committed by such subordinates under his or her command...(Section 15)

Prevention of Communal and Targeted Violence

Duty to prevent communal and targeted violence - Every public servant charged with the duty of maintenance of public order and tranquility including duties under sections 129 to 144A of the Code of Criminal Procedure, 1973, shall take all reasonable steps to prevent any act of communal and targeted violence including its build-up, incitement, outbreak and spread; and... (Section 18)

Penalties

The proposed legislation also provides for penalties/ punishment for the following offences:

Punishment for sexual assault - Whoever commits an act of sexual assault, shall be punishable

(a) where the act is contained in sub-clause (i) of clause (a) of Section 6 and clause (i) of clause (b) of Section 7, with rigorous imprisonment for a term which shall not be less than seven years but which may be for life and shall also be liable to fine.

(b) where the act is contained in section sub-clause (ii) of clause (a) of Section 7, with rigorous imprisonment for a term which shall not be less than ten years but which may be for life and shall also be liable to fine.

(c) where the act is contained in sub-clause (iii) of clause (a) of Section 7, rigorous imprisonment for a term a term which shall not be less than fourteen years but which may be for life and shall also be liable to fine.

(d) where the act is contained in sub-clauses (ii) to (vi) of clause (b) of Section 7, rigorous imprisonment for a term which shall not be less than seven years but which may extent to ten years and shall also be liable to fine. (Section 111)

Punishment for hate propaganda - The offence of hate propaganda shall be punishable with imprisonment which may extend to three years or fine or both. (Section 112)

Punishment for organised communal and targeted violence - Whoever commits organised communal and targeted violence shall be punished with rigorous imprisonment for life, and shall also be liable to fine. (Section 113)

Punishment for aiding financially, materially or in kind the commission of offence under this Act - Whoever is guilty of the offence under Section 10 shall be punished with imprisonment for a term, which may extend to three years, and shall also be liable to fine. (Section 114)

Punishment for torture – Whoever commits torture shall be punishable with rigorous imprisonment for a term which shall not be less than seven years but which may be for life and shall also be liable to fine. (Section 116)

Punishment for dereliction of duty - Whoever being a public servant is guilty of dereliction of duty shall be punished with imprisonment for two years which may extend to five years and shall be liable to fine. (Section 117)

Punishment for offences by public servants for breach of command responsibility - Whoever is guilty of an offence under Section 14 shall be punishable with rigorous imprisonment for life, when such failure relates to organised targeted violence and in any other case with imprisonment for a term of ten years and fine. (Section 118)

Punishment for offences by other superiors for breach of command responsibility - Whoever is guilty of an offence under section 15 shall be punishable with rigorous imprisonment for life, when such failure relates to organised targeted violence and in any other case with imprisonment for a term of ten years and fine. (Section 119)

Punishment for preparation - If any person makes preparation to do or omits to do anything which constitutes an offence punishable under this Act and from the circumstances of the case it may be reasonably inferred that he or she was determined to carry out his or her intention to commit the offence but had been prevented by circumstances independent of his or her will, he or she shall be punishable with rigorous imprisonment for a term which shall not be less than one-half of the minimum term (if any), but which may extend to...(Section 122)

Our purpose is not to write a full-fledged commentary on the proposed prospective legislation. Our purpose is to apprise the readers of essential features and some important provisions of the Bill so that the readers may appreciate the efficacy and role of such legislation in national integration.

(For further details please refer to the full text of the Bill included as Appendix 1 in the book).

Critical Analysis of the Proposed Prevention of Communal and Targeted Violence (Access to Justice and Reparations) Bill, 2011

Those opposing this Bill argue that it is an anti-majority Bill based on the assumption that the Hindus are always the perpetrators and they are never the victims of communal violence, and as such they do not require any protection. In that way, the Bill rests on the premise that India's religious and linguistic minorities and Scheduled Castes and Scheduled Tribes, who together constitute a formidable 40 per cent of the population, are likely to be the victims of targeted violence at the hands of the majority community, being 60 per cent of the total population. It is also being said that the Bill will harm federal structure of the Constitution, being more powers vested in the Central Government and that, too, at the cost of State governments. It is also being said that there is no cogent reason to presume that the majority community is always responsible for riots and a Bill based on such an unfounded presumption is a dangerous proposition. The word 'GROUP' as defined in Section 3 excludes majority community from its purview. There can't be two opinions about it that every law should be non-discriminatory, neutral and equally applicable to similarly situated persons. Fact of the matter is that both the communities suffer during communal violence. The only difference is that one suffers more and the other may suffer less. Were those who were burnt to death at Godhra railway station not Hindus? But it is also a fact so recorded in the reports of various fact finding committees and commissions appointed by the Central Government or State governments in this behalf and even otherwise it is common knowledge that Muslims are generally at the receiving end. Section 87 has been included in the Act to neutralise the effect of the exclusion of majority community from the purview of the term 'group' as defined in the Act which (Section 87) provides that any person whether or not he or she belongs to a group as defined under this Act, who has suffered physical, mental, psychological or monetary harm or harm to his or her property as a result of the commission of any offence under this Act, or when death has occurred as a consequence thereof, the next of kin of such deceased person shall be entitled to remedy and reparations including compensation, restitution and rehabilitation as applicable to them in accordance with the provisions under this chapter. Likewise, Section 89 also appears to have been included with the same intention. Section 89 provides that the State Government in co-ordination with the Chief-Secretary of the State, the Inspector General of Police, Superintendents of Police or Commissioner of Police, as the case may be, and the Collector shall ensure that any person mentioned under Section 87, whose life, liberty or property is threatened, or where he or she apprehends such threat, is immediately provided security, including creating police outposts and pickets in the vicinity of the affected area and providing temporary relocation, if necessary.

Some of the opponents of the Bill are also of the view that there is no need for more laws against communal violence and targeted violence in India because there are already many laws against hate speech and incitement of hate and violence. They feel that the laws seem to be too nebulous and not specific and what is needed is revision of the existing laws to some level of specificity, so that frivolous charges may not be made against innocent persons and those really involved in such nefarious activities do not go scot free and the charges can be framed if and when necessary only against the real culprits. They feel that the present-day situation does not warrant any new legislation.

The need of the hour is effective implementation of the existing laws. Present penal laws drafted more than hundred years ago during British period, undoubtedly, require revision, repeal or substitution and our law commission and legislative department of Ministry of Law and Justice are aware of it and follow up action is in progress.

Thus, the argument that no such law be made for providing protection to the minorities against communal violence does not hold water but the argument that the same yardstick should be applied to all viz., the majority community or minority communities, in such matters appears to be a valid argument. As a matter of fact, all riot victims be treated at par otherwise one may feel that minorities are bent upon bulldozing the majority community. It may also be described as a part of appeasement policy of any political party or parties (be in power or out of power).

It may be remembered that prevention of communal violence is a social issue and as such due weightage should be given to the views of all political parties whatever their ideology may be as also to the views of various social groups. Views of some political leaders representing different parties and social scientists representing different schools of thought, must not be considered in a haphazard manner. These views should be considered in proper perspective for arriving at a consensus. Consensus is inevitable in such matters because it will help in post-legislation exercise for changing the mind-set of the people without which it may not be possible to implement the law. Degree of success of dowry and environmental laws is still a debatable issue. Law can be imposed but imposition without acceptance by the masses has no meaning.

Law is a must to check growing menace of communal violence. Are the riots having taken place at the places mentioned above not sufficient to act upon? Enough is enough in a secular and civilised country like ours where a large number of people believe that even a small bird should not be killed what to talk of human beings. All of us must understand that there is no scope for the culture of impunity in a civilised society like ours, particularly for those who have no regard for human values and do not believe in *ahimsa* (non-violence). Those indulged in mass killings and their masters should not go unpunished and so the erring members of law enforcement agencies. Justice must be a fast moving exercise. It took two decades for rendering justice to the victims of bomb attacks in Mumbai in March 1993.

Thus the argument that slow pace of justice is limited to religious minorities only is also not sustainable. It is the common trend in our judicial institutions in all categories of cases what to talk of cases relating to victims of mass violence. Same is the story of 1984 Delhi riots, 1992 Gujarat riots, Meerut riots, etc.

Incidents of communal violence in India are generally dismissed as unfortunate events arising out of age-old enmity between different religious communities, though the ground situation has a different story to tell. In some of the riots, it has been proved beyond doubt that these they were well-orchestrated attacks which were otherwise not possible in the normal course.

Appendix

Prevention of Communal and Targeted Violence (Access to Justice and Reparations) BILL, 2011, pending before the Parliament and yet to become law.

CHAPTER I

PRELIMINARY

1. Short title, extent and commencement – (1) This Act is called "Prevention of Communal and Targeted Violence (Access to Justice and Reparations) Act, 2011".

(2) It extends to the whole of India, excluding the State of Jammu and Kashmir.

(3) It shall come into force within one year from the date of the passing of this Act.

2. Punishment of offences committed beyond, but which by law may be tried within, India - Any person liable under any Indian law, including this Act, to be tried for an offence committed beyond India shall be dealt in accordance with the provisions of this Act for any act committed beyond India in the same manner as if such act had been committed within India.

3. Definitions - In this Act, unless the context otherwise so requires:-

(a) "**Armed Forces or Security Forces**" means Armed Forces of the Union or Security Forces or Police Forces, as specified in Schedule I.

(b) "**Association**" means any combination or body of individuals, whether or not registered or incorporated under any law for the time being in force;

(c) "**Communal and targeted violence**" means and includes any act or series of acts, whether spontaneous or planned, resulting in injury or harm to the person and or property, knowingly directed against any person by virtue of his or her membership of any group.

(d) **"Fund"** means the Communal and Targeted Violence Relief and Rehabilitation Fund established under this Act;

(e) **"Group"** means a religious or linguistic minority, in any State in the Union of India, or Scheduled Castes and Scheduled Tribes within the meaning of clauses (24) and (25) of Article 366 of the Constitution of India;

(f) **"Hostile environment against a group** means an intimidating or coercive environment that is created when a person belonging to any group as defined under this Act, by virtue of his or her membership of that group, is subjected to any of the following acts:

(i) boycott of the trade or businesses of such person or making it otherwise difficult for him or her to earn a living; or,

(ii) publicly humiliate such person through exclusion from public services, including education, health and transportation or any act of indignity; or,

(iii) deprive or threaten to deprive such person of his or her fundamental rights; or,

(iv) force such person to leave his or her home or place of ordinary residence or livelihood without his or her express consent; or,

(v) any other act, whether or not it amounts to an offence under this Act, that has the purpose or effect of creating an intimidating, hostile or offensive environment.

(g) **"Internally displaced person"** means and includes any person, whether or not he or she belongs to a group as defined under this Act, who has been forced or obliged to leave his or her home or place of ordinary residence as a result of or in order to avoid the effects of organised communal or targeted violence to any other location within India. The term 'internal displacement' shall be construed accordingly;

(h) **"Prescribed"** means prescribed by rules or regulation, as the case may be, made under this Act;

(i) **"Public servant"** means a public servant as defined under section 21 of the Indian Penal Code, 1860 as well as any other person deemed to be a public servant under any other law including this Act for the time being in force and includes any person acting in his or her official capacity under the Central Government or the State Government;

(j) **"State"** shall carry the same meaning as in Article 1 of the Constitution of India read with Schedule I thereunder;

(k) **"Victim"** means any person belonging to a group as defined under this Act, who has suffered physical, mental, psychological or monetary harm or harm to his or her property as a result of the commission of any offence under this Act, and includes his or her relatives, legal guardian and legal heirs, wherever appropriate;

(l) **"Witness"** means person who is acquainted with the facts and circumstances, or is in possession of any information or has knowledge, necessary for the purpose of investigation, inquiry or trial of any crime involving an offence under this Act, and who is or may be required to give information or make a statement or produce any document during investigation, inquiry or trial of such case and includes a victim of such offence;

(m) All words and expressions used but not defined in the Act and defined in the Indian Penal Code 1860, the Indian Evidence Act 1872 or in the Code of Criminal Procedure 1973, as the case may be, shall be deemed to have the meanings assigned to them in the said enactments.

4. Knowledge–A person is said to knowingly direct any act against a person belonging to a group by virtue of such person's membership of that group where:

(a) he or she means to engage in the conduct against a person he or she knows belongs to that group; or,

(b) with the knowledge that the person belongs to a group, he or she means to cause injury or harm to such person because of the membership of such person to that group.

CHAPTER II

OFFENCES

5. Offences of communal and targeted violence- Offences under Section 7 to 12 (both inclusive) shall be offences of communal and targeted violence.

6. Applicability of SC/ST Atrocities Act- (1) In relation to offences against Scheduled Castes and Scheduled Tribes, this Act shall apply in addition and not in derogation of the Scheduled Castes and Scheduled Tribes (Prevention of Atrocities) Act, 1989 except to the extent mentioned in sub-Section (2) and (3).

(2) The provision of Rules 6 and 7 framed under the Scheduled Castes and Scheduled Tribes (Prevention of Atrocities) Rules, 1995 in relation to investigation of offences under the Scheduled Castes and Scheduled Tribes (Prevention of Atrocities) Act, 1989 shall apply to all investigation under that Act to the exclusion of Section 62 and section 85 of this Act.

(3) The provisions of Chapter VII of this Act shall apply to members of the Scheduled Castes and Scheduled Tribes against whom offences are committed under the Scheduled Castes and Scheduled Tribes (Prevention of Atrocities) Act, 1989 to the extent relevant.

Provided that any amounts paid under the said Act shall be set off against any amounts paid under this Act.

7. Sexual assault – A person is said to commit sexual assault if he or she commits any of the following acts against a person belonging to a group by virtue of that person's membership of a group:

(a) against a woman:

(i) rape

(ii) gang rape

(iii) rape or gang rape as part of or in the course of organised communal and targeted violence.

(b) against any person, without their consent or against their will,

(i) the introduction by a man of his penis or any other body part or an object into vagina, mouth or anus, to any extent;

(ii) causing harm or hurt to reproductive organs or genital organs;

(iii) exposing one's sexual organs in front of any person;

(iv) sexual contact of any sort, including the performance of sexual acts for any length of time;

(v) removing the persons clothes, partially or fully, or compelling that person to undress himself or herself, partially or fully, in public view or otherwise, or parading that person in undressed state in public view or otherwise;

(vi) any other act or conduct that subjects that person to sexual indignity.

Provided that where sexual assault under sub-Section (a) or (b) is committed as part of or in the course of organised communal and targeted violence, it shall not be necessary to prove that the said act was committed against the victim without their consent or against their will.

Explanation 1– For the purposes of this section, consent shall mean:

(a) The unequivocal voluntary agreement where the person has by words, gestures, or any form of non-verbal communication, communicated willingness to participate in the act referred to in this section; (b) "Unequivocal voluntary agreement" means willingness given for specific and be limited to the express act consented to under this section.

Explanation 2 – For the purposes of this section, consent obtained by duress, threat, terror, fear, coercion, undue influence, misrepresentation or mistake of fact shall not be unequivocal voluntary agreement.

8. Hate propaganda - Notwithstanding anything contained in any other law for the time being in force, whoever publishes, communicates or disseminates by words, either spoken or written, or by signs or by visible representation or by electronic or other means of mass communication or otherwise acts inciting hatred causing clear danger of violence against a group or persons belonging to that group, in general or specifically, or disseminates or broadcasts any information, or publishes or displays any advertisement or notice, that could reasonably be construed to demonstrate an intention to promote or incite hatred or expose or is likely to expose the group or persons belonging to that group to such hatred, is said to be guilty of hate propaganda.

Provided that nothing will be deemed to be hate propaganda, which is done in furtherance of or promotes fundamental rights enshrined in Chapter III of the Constitution of India.

9. Organised communal and targeted violence - (1) Whoever, being an individual, singly or jointly with others or being a part of an association or on behalf of an association or acting under the influence of an association, engages in continuing unlawful activity of a widespread or systematic nature knowingly directed against a group or part thereof, by virtue of their membership of that group, by use of violence or threat of violence or intimidation or coercion or by committing sexual assault or other unlawful means, is said to commit the offence of organised communal and targeted violence.

Explanation - For the purposes of this section, 'continuous unlawful activity of a widespread or systematic nature knowingly directed against a group or part thereof' means the course of conduct involving the multiple or mass commission of acts referred to in this section, whether spontaneously or planned, whether over a short or prolonged period or in one place or a number of places simultaneously or otherwise, against any group or part thereof.

(2) Where it is shown that continuing unlawful activity of a widespread or systematic nature has occurred, it may be presumed that the public servant charged with the duty to prevent communal and targeted violence has failed to act to prevent the widespread or systematic unlawful activity.

10. Aiding financially, materially or in kind for commission of offence under this Act - Whoever knowingly expends or supplies any money or any material or aids in kind thereof, in furtherance or in support of an act which is an offence under this Act is said to be guilty of aiding financially in the commission of an offence under this Act.

11. Offence under the Indian Penal Code, 1860 - The offences under the Indian Penal Code, 1860 provided in:

(a) Schedule II, Part A of this Act; or

(b) Schedule II, Part B of this Act, when committed against any person belonging to a group by virtue of his or her membership to that group, shall be deemed to be offences of communal and targeted violence under this Act and shall be dealt with accordingly.

12. Torture – Whoever, being a public servant, or under the control or direction of or with the acquiescence of a public servant, intentionally inflicts pain or suffering, whether mental or physical, or inflicts cruel, inhuman or degrading treatment, on a person belonging to a group by virtue of his or her membership of a group, including causing grievous hurt or danger to life, limb or health or sexual assault, for the purposes of obtaining from him or her or a third person information or a confession or punishing him or her for an act he or she or a third person committed or is suspected of having committed, or intimidating or coercing him or her or a third person or for any other purpose, is said to inflict torture.

Provided that nothing contained in this section shall apply to any pain, hurt or danger as aforementioned caused or inflicted in accordance with law.

13. Dereliction of duty - When any person who is or was a public servant not removable from his or her office save by or with the sanction of the Central Government or State Government, as the case may be, authorised to act under any provision of this Act:

(a) exercises the authority vested in him or her colourably or in a manner otherwise than provided under law for the time being in force, which causes or is likely to lead to an offence of communal and targeted violence or by which he or she intends to screen or knowing it to be likely that he or she will thereby screen any person from legal punishment; or,

(b) omits to exercise lawful authority vested in him or her under law, without reasonable cause, thereby fails to prevent the commission of communal and targeted violence, breach of public order or disruption in the maintenance of services and supplies essential to a group, shall be guilty of dereliction of duty.

Explanation - For the purpose of this Section, dereliction of duty shall also include the following:

(i) being charged as such public servant with the duty, who refuses to:

(a) protect or provide protection to any victim of communal and targeted violence;

(b) record any information under sub-Section (1) of Section 154, Code of Criminal Procedure, 1973 relating to the commission of any scheduled offence or any other offence under this Act; or prepares, frames or translates any document or electronic record incorrectly;

(c) investigate or prosecute any scheduled offence or any other offence under this Act;

(ii) being charged as such public servant, failing to perform his or her duties under Section 18 of this Act, to take all reasonable steps to prevent any act of communal and targeted violence including its build-up, incitement, outbreak and spread, and to discharge his or her duties without delay in a fair, impartial and non-discriminatory manner;

(iii) being charged as such public servant, failing to perform his or her duties under Section 63 of this Act, to conduct a medical examination without any delay in relation to a victim, who has suffered physical injury including sexual assault;

(iv) being charged as such public servant, failing to perform his or her duties under Section 65 of this Act, to take all reasonable steps to preserve relevant documents and records;

(v) being charged as such public servant, failing to perform his or her duties under Sections 66, 83 and 84 of this Act, to take all reasonable steps to protect victims, informants and witnesses;

(vi) furnishes false information on any issue within his or her purview and responsibility. If the information which the public servant is legally bound to give, is with respect to the commission of an offence under this Act, or is required for the purpose of preventing the commission of an offence under this Act.

(vii) exercises his or her legal authority corruptly or maliciously to register a false case against a person, or arrest or confine a person.

(viii) being legally bound as such public servant, intentionally omits to apprehend or to keep in confinement any person charged with or liable to be apprehended for an offence under this Act, or intentionally suffers such person to escape or intentionally aids such person in escaping.

(ix) knowingly or intentionally omits to furnish assistance that he or she is legally bound to provide to any public servant for the purpose of executing any process, summons or warrant lawfully issued by a Court of Justice, or of preventing the commission of an offence under this Act or of suppressing affray, or of apprehending a person charged with or guilty of an offence;

(x) where a public servant gives any information which he knows or believes to be false or suppresses any information or omits to give any information intending thereby to cause or knowing it to be likely that it will thereby cause injury or harm to any person belonging to a group.

(xi) being charged as such public servant, failing to take all reasonable steps to exercise duties under Chapter VII of under this Act; shall be guilty of dereliction of duty.

14. Offences by public servants for breach of command responsibility- (1) Whoever, being a public servant in command, control or supervision of the armed forces or security forces as defined under clause (a) of Section 3 of this Act or assuming command whether lawfully or otherwise, fails to exercise control over persons under his or her command, control, or supervision and as a result of such failure offences under this Act are committed, by persons under his or her command, control or supervision, or as a result of such failure the said persons fail to discharge their duties under this Act or any other law for the time being in force, shall be guilty of the offence of breach of command responsibility, where:-

(a) such public servant either knew or ought to have known having regard to the circumstances at the time that the persons under his or her command, control or supervision would commit or be likely to commit such offences; and,

(b) such public servant failed to take necessary and reasonable measures within his or her power to prevent or repress the commission of said offences or failed to submit the matter to the competent authorities for investigation and prosecution.

15. Offences by other superiors for breach of command responsibility - (1) Whoever, being any non-state actor or superior or office-bearer of any association as defined under clause (b) of Section 3 of this Act and other than those mentioned under Section 14, in command, control or supervision of any association or assuming command vested in him or her or otherwise, fails to exercise control over subordinates under his or her command, control, supervision and as a result of such failure offences under this Act are committed by subordinates under his or her command, control or supervision, shall be guilty of offences committed by such subordinates under his or her command, where:

(a) such non-state actor or superior or office-bearer of any association either knew, or consciously disregarded information which clearly indicated that his or her subordinates were committing or about to commit such offences;

(b) the offences concerned activities that were within the effective responsibility and control of such non-state actor or superior or office-bearer of any association; and

(c) such non-state actor or superior or office-bearer of any association failed to take all necessary and reasonable measures within his or her power to prevent or repress their commission or to submit the matter to the competent authorities for investigation and prosecution.

16. Superior orders and prescription of law - Where an offence has been committed under this Act, the fact that it was committed by a person pursuant to an order of a superior, shall not relieve that person of criminal responsibility unless:

(a) the person was under a legal obligation to obey orders of the superior in question; and

(b) the order was not manifestly unlawful.

17. Abetment of an offence - A person abets an offence, who –

First – Instigates any person to do that offence; or

Secondly – Engages with one or more other person or persons in any conspiracy for the doing of that offence, if an act or illegal omission takes place in pursuance of that conspiracy, and in order to the doing of that offence; or

Thirdly – Intentionally aids, by any act or illegal omission, the doing of that offence.

Explanation – A person who, by willful misrepresentation, or by willful concealment of a material fact, which he or she is bound to disclose, voluntarily causes or procures, or attempt to cause or procure a thing to be done, is said to instigate the doing of that offence.

Explanation 2 – Whoever, either prior to or at the time of commission of an act, does anything in order to facilitate the commission of that act, and thereby facilitates the commission thereof, is said to aid the doing of that act.

CHAPTER III

PREVENTION OF COMMUNAL AND TARGETED VIOLENCE

18. Duty to prevent communal and targeted violence - (1) Every public servant charged with the duty of maintenance of public order and tranquility including duties under Sections 129 to 144A of the Code of Criminal Procedure, 1973, shall take all reasonable steps to prevent any act of communal and targeted violence including its build-up, incitement, outbreak and spread; and to that end:

(i) make all possible efforts to identify patterns of violence in the State or any part thereof, that indicate occurrence of communal and targeted violence, including the creation or existence of hostile environment against a group;

(ii) obtain information regarding the likelihood of occurrence of communal or targeted violence; and,

(iii) act in furtherance of the duty to prevent communal and targeted violence in accordance with the powers vested in them;

(2) Every police officer shall take action, to the best of his or her ability, to prevent the commission of all offences under this Act.

(3) Every public servant exercising powers under this Act in discharge of his or her duties shall act without any delay in a fair, impartial and non-discriminatory manner.

19. Duty to exercise authority against unlawful assemblies - A public servant being charged with any duty under Sections 129 to 144A of the Code of Criminal Procedure, 1973 shall exercise his or her duty in a fair, impartial and non-discriminatory manner.

CHAPTER IV

NATIONAL AUTHORITY FOR COMMUNAL HARMONY, JUSTICE AND REPARATION

20. Constitution of National Authority for Communal Harmony, Justice and Reparation - (1) The Central Government shall constitute a body known as the National Authority for Communal Harmony, Justice and Reparation to exercise the powers and perform the functions assigned to it under this Act.

(2) The National Authority shall be a body corporate with the name aforesaid having perpetual succession and a common seal with the power, subject to the provisions of this Act to acquire, hold and dispose of property and to contract, and may, by the aforesaid name, sue or be sued.

(3) The National Authority shall consist of a Chairperson, a Vice-Chair-person and five other Members.

Provided that, at all times, not less than four Members, including the Chairperson and Vice-Chairperson, shall belong to a group as defined under this Act.

Provided further that, at all times, there shall be:

1. one member belonging to Scheduled Castes or Scheduled Tribes;
2. four women, whether Chairperson, Vice-Chairperson or Member;

Provided further that, at all times, one woman, whether Chairperson, Vice-Chairperson or Member, shall belong to a religious or linguistic minority.

Provided further that, at all times, not more than two Members, including the Chairperson and Vice-Chairperson, shall be retired public servants.

(4) There shall be a Secretary-General, who shall be an officer of the rank of the Secretary to the Government of India, appointed in consultation with the Chairperson of the National Authority, who shall be the Chief Executive Officer of the National Authority and shall exercise such powers and discharge such functions of the National Authority as it may delegate to him or her.

(5) The headquarters of the National Authority shall be at Delhi and the Authority may, with the previous approval of the Central Government, establish offices at other places in India.

21. Appointment of Chairperson, Vice-Chairperson and other Members - (1) The Chairperson, Vice-Chairperson and Members shall be appointed by the President by warrant under his or her hand and seal:

Provided that every appointment under this sub-section shall be made after obtaining the recommendations of a Selection Committee consisting of:

(i) The Prime Minister - **Chairperson**

(ii) Leader of the Opposition in the House of the People - **Member**

(iii) Leader of the Opposition in the Council of States - **Member**

(iv) Minister in-charge of the Ministry of Home Affairs in the Government of India - **Member**

(v) Chairperson of National Human Rights Commission - **Member**

Explanation 1 - For the purposes of this sub-Section, "the Leader of the Opposition in the House of the People" shall, when no such Leader has been so recognised, include the Leader of the single largest group in opposition of the Government in the House of the People.

Explanation 2 - For the purposes of this sub-Section, "the Leader of the Opposition in the Council of States" shall, when no such Leader has been so recognised, include the Leader of the single largest group in opposition of the Government in the Council of States.

(2) The process of selection shall be initiated by the office of the Prime Minister of India within three months of the coming into force of this Act in the first instance and three months prior to the completion of tenure of the existing Chairperson, Vice-Chairperson or Member and shall be concluded within two months.

(3) The decisions of the Selection Committee shall be by a simple majority.

22. Qualifications - (1) The Chairperson, Vice-Chairperson and Members of the National Authority shall have the following qualifications and shall be chosen from amongst persons:

(a) having expertise in relation to law or criminal justice or human rights or sociology or any other related social science;

(b) having a record of promoting communal harmony;

(c) being of high moral character, impartiality and integrity; and,

(d) who have not been members of any political party for a period of one year prior to their selection.

(2) No person shall be eligible to be appointed as a Chairperson, Vice-Chairperson or Member of the National Authority if:

(a) an inquiry into an offence under any law for the time being in force, including any offence provided under the Prevention of Corruption Act, 1988, is pending against him or her or he or she has been convicted for such offence;

(b) he or she has, in any manner, exhibited bias against any group, by acts or in writing or otherwise; or

(c) if subject to any disciplinary control, whether a public servant or otherwise, a disciplinary proceeding is pending against him or her, or he or she has been found guilty in any such proceeding.

(3) The Chairperson, Vice-Chairperson and Members of the National Authority shall not contest elections for a period of two years after completion of their term either under the Government of India or under the Government of any State except to the office of President or Vice President of the Union of India.

23. Term of office of Members - (1) The Members of the National Authority shall serve on a full-time basis for a six years term.

Provided that at the first selection, two members shall be appointed for a term of two years, two members for a term of four years, and the remainder appointed for a term of six years.

(2) A person appointed as Chairperson or Vice-Chairperson shall hold office for a term of two years from the date on which he or she enters upon his or her office.

(3) A person appointed as Chairperson or Vice-Chairperson shall not be eligible for re-appointment in the same capacity.

(4) Except at the first instance, members with two years service in the National Authority alone will be qualified to be Chairperson or Vice Chairperson.

24. Resignation and removal of Chairperson, Vice-Chairperson and Members - (1) The Chairperson, Vice-Chairperson or any Member may, by notice in writing under his or her hand addressed to the President of India, resign from his or her office.

(2) Subject to the provisions of sub-Section (2) of Section 22, the Chairperson, the Vice-Chairperson or any Member of the National Authority shall only be removed from his or her office by order of the President on the grounds of proven misbehaviour or functional incapacity after the Supreme Court in a reference made to it by the President, has on inquiry, held, in accordance with the procedure prescribed in that behalf that the person ought on any such ground be removed.

(3) Notwithstanding anything sub-Section (2), the President may by order remove from office the Chairperson, Vice-Chairperson or any other Member if the Chairperson, Vice-Chairperson or any other Member, as the case may be :

(a) engages during his or her term of office in any paid employment outside the duties of his or her office; or

(b) is unfit to continue in office by reasons of infirmity of mind or body; or

(c) is convicted and sentenced to imprisonment for an offence which in the opinion of the President involves moral turpitude.

25. Vacancies in the Authority - (1) No act or proceedings of the National Authority shall be questioned or shall be invalidated merely on the ground of existence of any vacancy or defect in the constitution of the National Authority.

(2) In the event of the occurrence of any vacancy in the office of the National Authority caused by any reason, a selection shall be held in accordance with Section 21 to fill the vacancy within two months of the vacancy arising.

(3) A member so appointed to fill a vacancy shall serve for the remainder of the predecessor's term and, if that period is two years or less, shall be eligible for re-selection for a full term.

26. Terms and conditions of service of Chairperson, Vice-Chairperson and Members - The salaries and allowances payable to, and other terms and conditions of services of the Chairperson, Vice-Chairperson and Members shall be such as may be prescribed.

Provided that neither the salary and allowances nor the other terms and conditions of service of the Chairperson, Vice-Chairperson or any Member shall be varied to his or her disadvantage during his or her tenure.

27. Procedure to be regulated by the National Authority - (1) Subject to the provisions of this Act and the rules made thereunder, the National Authority shall have the power to lay down its own procedure.

(2) All orders and decisions of the National Authority shall be authenticated by the Secretary-General or any other officer of the National Authority duly authorised by the Chairperson in this behalf.

28. Officers and other staff of the National Authority - (1) The Central Government shall make available to the National Authority such police and investigative staff under an officer not below the rank of a Director General of Police and such other officers and staff as the National Authority may deem necessary for the efficient performance of its functions.

(2) Subject to such rules as may be made by the Central Government in this behalf, the National Authority may appoint such other administrative, technical staff as it may consider necessary.

(3) The salaries, allowances and conditions of service of the officers and other staff appointed under sub-Section (2) shall be such as may be prescribed.

(4) The National Authority shall perform its functions on its own or through the State Authorities appointed under this Act, or through any persons appointed by it or through such other procedures and mechanisms it may adopt.

29. Functions of the National Authority - The National Authority shall perform all or any of the following functions, namely:

(a) receive and collect information on:

(i) any acts that indicate a build up by State or non-state actors of offences under this Act;

(ii) any form of communication, propaganda, mobilisation or the activities of persons, which may promote enmity or hatred against groups;

(iii) occurrence or likely occurrence of offences of communal and targeted violence in the manner prescribed by rules under this Act;

(iv) negligence in the prevention of communal and targeted violence by public servants.

(b) entertain appeals against decisions of the State Assessment Committee in relation to non-inclusion of names of persons under section 95.

(c) issue advisories and make recommendations, in relation to clause (a) above and section 30, to State and non-state actors;

(d) frame, in consultation with the Central Government, schemes for making reparations to all persons entitled under Section 87 including those registered under Section 95;

(e) frame, in consultation with the Central Government, guidelines in relation to the prevention and control of communal and targeted violence;

(f) receive regular reports at least once every quarter on incidents, outbreaks and patterns of communal and targeted violence from all State Authorities constituted under this Act;

(g) visit, under intimation to the State Government, any relief camp under the control of the State Government, where internally displaced persons reside, to review the living conditions of such persons;

(h) visit, under intimation to the Central Government or the State Government, any jails or any other institution under the control of the Central Government or the State Government, as the case may be, where persons are detained or lodged for the purposes of inquiry or investigation into any offence under this Act;

(i) observe proceedings in court in relation to any offence punishable under this Act either through Members of the State Authority or by appointing independent observers;

(j) intervene in any proceeding, involving any allegation of communal and targeted violence pending before a court, with approval of such court;

(k) such other functions that it may consider necessary for the preservation of communal harmony and prevention and control of communal and targeted violence.

Provided that where any State Authority has commenced an inquiry under powers vested under this Act, the National Authority shall not inquire into the same.

Provided further that the National Authority shall inquire into complaints of organised communal and targeted violence and no State Authority shall have the power to inquire into such complaints.

30. Monitoring and Review by National Authority of Performance of Duties - The National Authority shall observe, monitor and review the performance of duties by public servants in relation to the following:

(i) effectiveness of steps taken by public servant for prevention of offences of communal and targeted violence;

(ii) recording of information where offences under this Act have been committed by public servants;

(iii) timely and effective investigation and prosecution of offences under this Act, including offences by public servants;

(iv) provision of timely and adequate measures related to relief, rehabilitation, reparation and restitution of all persons entitled to such benefits under Section 87 including those registered under Section 95, in accordance with provisions of this Act.

31. Powers of the National Authority - (1) The National Authority in the fulfillment of its objectives and in furtherance of its functions shall have the following powers, namely:

(a) requisitioning information from the:

(i) Central government, any State government or concerned Union Territory or any of their officers or departments; or

(ii) non-state actors;

(b) appointing any person to observe, gather facts and information, inquire on its behalf;

(c) issue directions to State Authorities in relation to the conduct of any inquiry.

Provided that any direction issued by the National Authority to any State Authority shall be binding on the State Authority.

(2) The National Authority shall, while inquiring or investigating, have the powers of a Civil Court trying a suit under the Code of Civil Procedure, 1908, in respect of the following matters, namely:

(a) summoning and enforcing the attendance of witnesses and examining them on oath;

(b) discovery and production of any document;

(c) receiving evidence on affidavits;

(d) issuing commissions for the examination of witnesses or documents;

(e) any other matter which may be prescribed.

(3) The National Authority shall have power to require any person, subject to any privilege which may be claimed by that person under any law for the time being in force, to furnish information on such matters as, in the opinion of the Authority, may be useful or relevant to, the inquiry and any person so required shall be deemed to be legally bound to furnish such information within the meaning of Section 176 and section 177 of the Indian Penal Code.

(4) The National Authority through any other Gazetted Officer specially authorised in this behalf by the National Authority may enter any building or place where the National Authority has reason to believe that any document relating to the subject matter of the inquiry or investigation may be found, and may enter and seize any such document or take extracts or copies there from subject to the provisions of section 100, Code of Criminal Procedure, 1973, in so far as it may be applicable.

(5) The National Authority shall be deemed to be a civil court and when any offence as is described in Section 175, Section 178, Section 179, Section 180 or Section 228 of the Indian Penal Code, 1860 is committed in the view or presence of the Authority, the Authority may, after recording the facts constituting the offence and the statement of the accused as provided for in the Code of Criminal Procedure, 1973, forward the case to a Magistrate or the Designated Judge as the case may be, having jurisdiction to try the same and the Magistrate or the Designated Judge to whom any such case is forwarded shall proceed to hear the complaint against the accused as if the case has been forwarded to him under Section 346, Code of Criminal Procedure, 1973.

(6) Every proceeding in relation to an inquiry or investigation before the National Authority shall be deemed to be a judicial proceeding within the meaning of Sections 193 and 228, and for the purposes of Section 196, of the Indian Penal Code, and the Authority shall be deemed to be a civil court for all the purposes of Section 195 and Chapter XXVI of the Code of Criminal Procedure, 1973.

32. Investigation - (1) The National Authority may, for the purpose of conducting any investigation pertaining to the inquiry, utilise the services of any officer or investigation agency of the Central Government or any State Government with the concurrence of the Central Government or the State Government, as the case may be.

(2) For the purpose of investigating into any matter pertaining to the inquiry, any officer or agency whose services are utilised under sub-Section (1) may, subject to the direction and control of the National Authority –

(a) summon and enforce the attendance of any person and examine him;

(b) require the discovery and production of any document; and

(c) requisition any public record or copy thereof from any office.

(3) The provision of Section 40 shall apply in relation to any statement made by a person before any officer or agency whose services are utilised under sub-Section (1) as they apply in relation to any statement made by a person in the course of giving evidence before the National Authority.

(4) The officer or agency whose services are utilised under sub-Section (1) shall investigate into any matter pertaining to the inquiry and submit a report thereon to the National Authority within such period as may be specified by the National Authority in this behalf.

(5) The National Authority shall satisfy itself about the correctness of the facts stated and the conclusion, if any, arrived at in the report submitted to it under sub-Section (4) and for this purpose the National Authority may make such inquiry (including the examination of the person or persons who conducted or assisted in the investigation) as it thinks fit.

33. Inquiry into complaints - The National Authority while inquiring into the complaints of offences under this Act may –

(i) Call for information or report from the Central Government or any State Government or any other authority or organisation subordinate thereto within such time as may be specified by it:

Provided that –

(a) If the information or report is not received within the time stipulated by the National Authority, it may proceed to inquire into the complaint on its own;

(b) If, on receipt of information or report, the National Authority is satisfied either that no further inquiry is required or that the required action has been initiated or taken by the concerned Government or authority, it may not proceed with the complaint and inform the complainant accordingly;

(ii) without prejudice to anything contained in clause (i), if it considers necessary, having regard to the nature of the complaint, initiate an inquiry.

34. Steps after inquiry - The National Authority may take any of the following steps upon the completion of an inquiry held under this Act, namely,

(1) where the inquiry discloses violations of the provisions of this Act or negligence in the prevention of communal and targeted violence by a public servant, it may recommend to the concerned Government or authority the initiation of proceedings for prosecution or such other action as the National Authority may deem fit against the concerned person or persons;

(2) approach the Supreme Court or the High Court concerned for such directions, orders or writs as that Court may deem necessary;

(3) the National Authority shall send a copy of its inquiry report together with its recommendations to the concerned Government or authority and the concerned government or authority shall, within a period of one month, or such further time as the National Authority may allow, forward its comments on the report, including the action taken or proposed to be taken thereon, to the National Authority;

(4) The National Authority shall publish its inquiry report together with the comments of the concerned government or authority, if any, and the action taken or proposed to be taken by the concerned Government or authority on the recommendations of the National Authority.

35. Copy of inquiry report to be given to complainant - It shall be the duty of the National Authority to provide a copy of the inquiry report under sub-Section (3) of Section 34 to the complainant or his or her representative.

36. Procedure with respect to armed forces or security forces - (1) Notwithstanding anything contained in this Act, while dealing with complaints of offences under this Act by members of the armed forces or security forces, the National Authority shall adopt the following procedures, namely:

(a) it may, either on its own motion or on receipt of a petition, seek a report from the Central Government;

(b) after the receipt of the report, it may, either not proceed with the complaint or, as the case may be, make its recommendations to that government.

(2) The Central Government shall inform the National Authority of the action taken on the recommendations within three months or such further time as the National Authority may allow.

(3)The National Authority shall publish its report together with its recommendations made to the Central Government and the Action taken by the Government on such recommendations.

(4) The National Authority shall provide a copy of the report published under sub-Section (3) to the complainant or his or her representative.

37. Duty to respond to advisories or recommendations of the National Authority - It shall be the duty of the Central Government, the State Government and public servant at all levels, to take appropriate action on all advisories and recommendations issued to them by the National Authority under clause (c) of Section 29 and submit an Action Taken Report within thirty days.

Provided that in the event of any disagreement with the advisories or recommendations of the National Authority, the appropriate government or the public servant shall give reasons in writing to the National Authority within seven days of the receipt of the advisory or recommendation.

38. Identity of victim and informant to be protected - The National Authority shall take appropriate action to protect the identity of the victim or informant at all times.

39. Statutory Information - (1) It shall be the duty of any District Magistrate or Police Commissioner having knowledge or information of patterns and incidents of outbreaks of communal and targeted violence or anticipating any of these, to report to the National Authority in writing without any delay.

(2) All reports received by the Ministry of Home Affairs, the Home Departments of all State Governments, and District Magistrates relating to communal and targeted violence, build-up and possibilities thereof and advisories related therein shall be sent to the National Authority without any delay.

40. Statements made by persons to the National Authority - No statement made by a person in the course of giving evidence before the National Authority, shall subject him or her to, or be used against him or her in, any civil or criminal proceedings;

Provided that the statement –

(i) is made in reply to the question which he or she is required by the National Authority to answer; or

(ii) is relevant to the subject matter of the inquiry.

41. Annual Report - (1) The National Authority shall prepare an Annual Report giving details of:

(a) all specific advisories and recommendations issued by the National Authority under this Act;

(b) details of compliance or non-compliance with the advisories, and recommendations of the National Authority, by the Central or State Government along with reasons for the same; and,

(c) details of any other guideline, programme or activity performed by the National Authority during the year.

(2) The Annual Report shall be tabled in the Parliament in the monsoon session of each calendar year.

CHAPTER V

STATE AUTHORITIES FOR COMMUNAL HARMONY, JUSTICE AND REPARATION

42. Constitution of State Authorities for Communal Harmony, Justice and Reparation - (1) Each State Government shall constitute a body to be known as the … (name of State) State Authority for Communal Harmony, Justice and Reparation, to exercise the powers conferred upon, and to perform the functions assigned to a State Authority under this Act.

(2) The State Authority shall be a body corporate with the name aforesaid having perpetual succession and a common seal with the power, subject to the provisions of this Act to acquire, hold and dispose of property and to contract, and may, by the aforesaid name, sue or be sued.

(3) The State Authority shall, with effect from such date as the State Government may by notification specify, consist of a Chairperson, a Vice-Chair-person and five other Members.

Provided that, at all times, not less than four Members, including the Chairperson and Vice-Chairperson, shall belong to a group as defined under this Act.

Provided further that, at all times, there shall be -

1. one Member belonging to Scheduled Castes or Scheduled Tribes;
2. four women, whether Chairperson, Vice-Chairperson or Member;

Provided further that, at all times, one woman, whether Chairperson, Vice-Chairperson or Member, shall belong to a religious or linguistic minority.

Provided further that, at all times, not more than two Members, including the Chairperson and Vice-Chairperson, shall be retired public servants.

(4) There shall be a Secretary, who shall be an officer of the rank of the Secretary to the Government of the State, appointed in consultation with the Chairperson of the State Authority, who shall be the Chief Executive Officer and shall exercise such powers and discharge such functions of the State Authority as it may delegate to him or her.

(5) The headquarters of the State Authority shall be at such place as the State Government may, by notification, specify.

43. Appointment of Chairperson, Vice-Chairperson and Members of the State Authority - (1) The Chairperson, Vice-Chairperson and Members of the State Authority shall be appointed by the Governor by warrant under his or her hand and seal:

Provided that every appointment under this sub-Section shall be made after obtaining the recommendation of a Committee consisting of:

(i) The Chief Minister of the State - **Chairperson**

(ii) Leader of Opposition in the Legislative Assembly of the State - **Member**

(iii) Leader of Opposition in the Legislative Council of the State - **Member**

(iv) Minister in-charge of the Ministry of Home Affairs in the Government of the State **Member**

(v) Chairperson of the State Human Rights Commission - **Member**

Provided further that in States that do not have a Legislative Council, the Speaker of the Legislative Assembly shall be a member of the Selection Committee.

Explanation 1- For the purposes of this sub-Section, "Leader of the Opposition in the Legislative Assembly of the State" shall, when no such Leader has been so recognised, include the Leader of the single largest group in opposition of the Government in the Legislative Assembly.

Explanation 2 - For the purposes of this sub-Section, "the Leader of the Opposition in the Legislative Council" shall, when no such Leader has been so recognised, include the Leader of the single largest group in opposition of the Government in the Legislative Council.

(2) The process of selection shall be initiated by the State Government within three months of its constitution in the first instance and three months prior to the completion of tenure of the existing State Authority and shall be concluded within three months.

(3) The decisions of the Selection Committee shall be by majority.

44. Qualifications - (1) The Chairperson, Vice-Chairperson and Members of the State Authority shall have the following qualifications and shall be chosen from amongst persons:

(a) having expertise in relation to law or criminal justice or human rights or sociology or any other related social science;

(b) having a record of promoting communal harmony;

(c) being of high moral character, impartiality and integrity; and,

(d) who have not been members of any political party for a period of one year prior to their selection.

(2) No person shall be eligible to be appointed as a Chairperson, Vice-Chairperson or Member of the State Authority if:

(a) an inquiry into an offence under any law for the time being in force, including any offence provided under the Prevention of Corruption Act, 1988, is pending against him or her or he or she has been convicted for such offence;

(b) he or she has, in any manner, exhibited bias against any group, by acts or in writing or otherwise; or

(c) if subject to any disciplinary control, whether a public servant or otherwise, a disciplinary proceeding is pending against him or her, or he or she has been found guilty in any such proceeding.

(3) The Chairperson, Vice-Chairperson and Members of the State Authority shall not contest elections for a period of two years after completion of their term either under the Governmentof India or under the

Government of any State except to the office of President or Vice President of the Union of India.

45. Terms of the Members of the State Authority - (1) The Members of the State Authority shall serve on a full-time basis for a six years term.

Provided that at the first selection, two members shall be appointed for a term of two years, two members for a term of four years, and the remainder appointed for a term of six years.

(2) A person appointed as Chairperson or Vice-Chairperson shall hold office for a term of two years from the date on which he or she enters upon his or her office.

(3) A person appointed as Chairperson or Vice-Chairperson shall not be eligible for re-appointment in the same capacity.

(4) Except for the first election, members with two years service in the State Authority alone will be qualified to be Chairperson or Vice Chairperson.

46. Resignation and removal of Chairperson, Vice-Chairperson and Members - (1) The Chairperson, Vice-Chairperson or any Member may, by notice in writing under his or her hand addressed to the Governor of the State, resign from his or her office.

(2) Subject to the provisions of sub-Section (2) of Section 44, the Chairperson, the Vice-Chairperson or any Member of the National Authority shall only be removed from his or her office by order of the President on the grounds of proven misbehaviour or functional incapacity after the Supreme Court in a reference made to it by the President, has on inquiry, held, in accordance with the procedure prescribed in that behalf that the person ought on any such ground be removed.

(3) Notwithstanding anything sub-Section (2), the President may by order remove from office the Chairperson, Vice-Chairperson or any other Member if the Chairperson, Vice-Chairperson or any other Member, as the case may be -

(a) engages during his or her term of office in any paid employment outside the duties of his or her office; or

(b) is unfit to continue in office by reasons of infirmity of mind or body; or

(c) is convicted and sentenced to imprisonment for an offence which in the opinion of the President involves moral turpitude.

47. Vacancies in the State Authority - (1) No act or proceedings of the State Authority shall be questioned or shall be invalidated merely on the ground of existence of any vacancy or defect in the constitution of the State Authority.

(2) In the event of the occurrence of any vacancy in the office of the State Authority caused by any reason, a selection shall be held in accordance with Section 43 to fill the vacancy within two months of the vacancy arising.

(3) A Member so appointed to fill a vacancy shall serve for the remainder of the predecessor's term and, if that period is two years or less, shall be eligible for re-selection for a full term.

48. Terms and conditions of service of Chairperson, Vice-Chairperson and Members of the State Authority - The salaries and allowances payable to, and other terms and conditions of services of the Chairperson, Vice-Chairperson and Members shall be such as may be prescribed by the State Government.

Provided that neither the salary and allowances nor the other terms and conditions of service of the Chairperson, Vice-Chairperson or a Member shall be varied to his or her disadvantage after his or her appointment.

49. Procedure to be regulated by the State Authority - (1) Subject to the provisions of this Act and the rules made thereunder, the State Authority shall have the power to lay down, its own procedure.

(2) All orders and decisions of the State Authority shall be authenticated by the Secretary or any other officer of the State Authority duly authorised by the Chairperson of the State Authority in this behalf.

50. Officers and other staff of the State Authority - (1) The State Government shall make available to the State Authority such police and investigative staff under an officer not below the rank of Inspector General of Police and such other officers and staff as may be necessary for the efficient performance of the functions of the State Authority.

(2) Subject to such rules as may be made by the State Government in this behalf, the State Authority may appoint such other administrative, technical staff as it may consider necessary.

(3) The salaries, allowances and conditions of service of the officers and other staff appointed under sub-Section (2) shall be such as may be prescribed by the State Government.

51. Functions of the State Authority - The State Authority shall perform all or any of the following functions on its own or through persons appointed by it, namely:-

(a) receive and collect information, through any means in whatsoever manner including under directions issued by the National Authority, on:

(i) any acts that indicate a build up by State or non-state actors towards communal and targeted violence;

(ii) any form of communication, propaganda, mobilisation or the activities of persons, which may promote enmity or hatred against groups.

(b) issue advisories and recommendations to State and non-state actors in relation to clause (a) and Section 52;

provided that where the information received pertains to organised communal and targeted violence, the State Authority

52. Monitoring and review by State Authority of performance of duties - The State Authority shall observe, monitor and review the performance of duties by public servants in relation to the following:

(i) effectiveness of steps taken by public servant for prevention of communal and targeted violence;

(ii) recording of information where offences under this Act have been committed;

(iii) provision of timely and adequate measures related to relief, rehabilitation, reparation and restitution of all persons entitled under Section 87 including those registered under Section 95, in accordance with provisions of this Act.

53. Application of certain provisions relating to the National Authority to the State Authority - The provisions of Section 31 shall apply to a State Authority and shall have effect,

subject to the modification that references to "National Authority" shall be construed as references to "State Authority".

54. Defender for Justice and Reparations - (1) The State Authority may invite nominations from non-governmental organisations, civil society or individuals to appoint, for each district, such number of non-governmental organisations or individuals as it may be necessary, who shall be known as the 'Human Rights Defender for Justice and Reparations' to perform the functions assigned to it under this Act.

(2) The nominations received under sub-Section (1) shall be duly examined by the State Authority to appoint a Human Rights Defender for Justice and Reparations for a period of three years and who shall be a non-governmental organisation or individual who has expertise in relation to law or human rights and has a record of preserving communal harmony.

(3) The Human Rights Defender for Justice and Reparations shall function to ensure that all persons, whether or not they belong to a group as defined under this Act, affected by communal and targeted violence and entitled to benefits under Section 87, are able to access their rights under the Constitution of India or this Act or any other law for the time being in force, and for the aforesaid purpose, do all such things as may be necessary to achieve that objective of access to justice.

(4) The Human Rights Defender for Justice and Reparations may bring to the notice of the concerned State Authority any act or omission that amounts to an offence under this Act and shall strive towards building and maintaining communal harmony.

CHAPTER VI

INVESTIGATION, PROSECUTION AND TRIAL

55. Application of Code of Criminal Procedure, 1973 - Provisions of the Code of Criminal Procedure, 1973, shall apply to this Act, save and except as amended or supplemented to the extent provided under this Chapter, in relation to offences committed under this Act.

56. Offences to be cognizable and non-bailable - Unless otherwise specified under Schedule I of the Code of Criminal Procedure, 1973, all offences specified under this Act, shall be cognizable and non-bailable.

57. Translated true copy of information to be given within seven days – (1) A true translated copy of information recorded under sub-section (2) of Section 154 of the Code of Criminal Procedure, 1973, shall be supplied forthwith, free of cost, to the informant or victim in the language understood by him or her.

(2) Where any information is received through electronic communication including electronic mail or fax, such electronic communication shall be recorded fully and accurately in such a manner that the original content of such electronic communication is not lost in translation and a copy of such electronic communication shall be appended to the true translated copy of information recorded and supplied to the informant or victim under sub-Section (1).

58. Inaccurate recording of information - Any informant who believes that the information referred to in sub-section (1) of section 154 of the Code of Criminal Procedure, 1973 was not recorded accurately or fully, or who fails to get a copy of the recorded information if submitted orally or through electronic communication, may send the substance of such information, in writing and by post, to the concerned Superintendant of Police or Deputy Commissioner of Police as the case may be, who, if satisfied that such information discloses the commission of an offence under this Act, shall either investigate the case himself or herself or direct an investigation to be made by an police officer subordinate to him or her, in the manner provided under this Act, and such officer shall have all the powers of an officer in-charge of the station in relation to that offence.

59. Recording of information in relief camps - (1) It shall be the duty of a police officer not below the rank of Deputy Superintendent of Police to visit every relief camp within three days of its establishment to conduct an inquiry and record statements into the circumstances and cause of each individual being displaced and put in a relief camp.

(2) The statements under sub-Section (1) shall be recorded in the presence of two respectable citizens belonging to the same group as the informant or victim and must be attested by them and all such statements

shall be treated as being statements under sub-Section (3) of Section 161 of the Code of Criminal Procedure, 1973.

Provided that where the victim of sexual assault is a woman or child, the information shall be recorded by a Deputy Superintendent of Police or Assistant Commissioner of Police, as the case may be, who is a woman.

Provided further that where any statement recorded under this Section discloses a cognizable offence, it shall be deemed to be information recorded under section 154, Code of Criminal Procedure, 1973.

60. Investigation by Senior Police Officers - No police officer below the rank of Deputy Superintendent of Police or Assistant Commissioner of Police, as the case may be, shall investigate any offence contained in Sections 7 to 17 (both inclusive) of this Act.

61. Women Police Officers - Where the offence of sexual assault is committed against a woman or a child, the investigation, as far as possible, shall be conducted by a woman police officer.

62. Recording of statements or evidence during investigation - (1) The Investigating Officer may, during investigation into any offence under this Act, produce the victim or the informant, when such informant is victim, before a Metropolitan Magistrate or a Judicial Magistrate, as the case may be, for recording his or her statement under Section 164 of the Code of Criminal Procedure, 1973.

Provided that the victim shall have the right to have his or her advocate present at the time of recording of such statement and a copy of the statement so recorded should be provided to him or her.

(2) Any statement of a person other than the person mentioned in sub-Section (1) may be recorded by the Investigating Officer under Section 161 of the Code of Criminal Procedure, 1973 or by the Metropolitan Magistrate or Judicial Magistrate under section 164 thereof, as the case may be.

(3) Any Metropolitan Magistrate or Judicial Magistrate may, whether or not he or she has territorial jurisdiction in the case, shall on a request, record any statement under Section 164 of the Code of Criminal Procedure, 1973 or receive affidavit from any victim, informant or witnesses made to him or her during the investigation under this Act but before the commencement of the inquiry or trial:

(a) Any statement (other than a confession) made under sub-Section (2) shall be recorded in the manner provided for the recording of evidence, or in the opinion of the said Magistrate best suited to the circumstances of the case; and the said Magistrate shall have the power to administer oath to the person whose statement is so recorded.

(b) The Magistrate recording a statement under this section shall forward it to the Designated Judge by whom the case is to be inquired into or tried.

(4) The victim, informant or witness may also send such statement to the National Authority or the State Authority for necessary action.

63. Medical Examination of victim - (1) For investigation of offences under this Act causing any physical injury to a victim, the medical examination shall be conducted without any delay by at least two registered medical practitioners employed in a hospital run by the government or a local authority and in the absence of such practitioners by any other registered medical practitioners, with the consent of such victim or of a person competent to give such consent on behalf of the victim.

(2) In cases of sexual assault, the medical examination shall be conducted by at least two registered medical practitioners of whom one shall be a woman in the manner prescribed under Section 164A of the Code of Criminal Procedure, 1973 and the expression "woman" thereunder shall be read to include a "man".

(3) For investigation of offences under this Act resulting in death, the post-mortem shall be conducted by a Board consisting of three registered medical practitioners one of whom shall be a woman.

(4) The post-mortem conducted under sub-Section (3) shall be done in the presence of a representative of the victim if so requested by him or her and the entire procedure shall be videographed and photographed and a copy of which shall be attached with the Medical Report. The copy of the report of the medical examination under sub-Section (1) and (2) or report of the post-mortem under sub-Section (3), shall be given within forty-eight hours of completion of the medical examination or post-mortem, to the investigating agency and the victim or his or her representatives, as the case may be.

Provided that where chemical analysis is done, the report of the chemical analysis shall be made available to the investigating agency and the victim within fifteen days.

64. Videographic and photographic evidence - The collection of evidence relating to an offence under this Act shall include videographing and or photographing of the scene of crime and the same shall form a part of the report of the case under Section 173 of the Code of Criminal Procedure, 1973.

Provided that in the event of any failure to record such evidence, the same shall not vitiate the trial in any manner.

65. Preservation of records and documents - (1) Where any offence under this Act has been committed, the concerned police officer within whose jurisdiction such offence has been committed shall preserve records including records of the police control room, case diary, station diary or any other record that is in any way concerned with the investigation of the offence.

(2) Where any offence under this Act has been committed, the Superintendent of Police, within whose jurisdiction such offence has been committed, shall notify all hospitals, whether public or private, to preserve all medical and hospital records and all such hospitals shall be bound to preserve such records.

(3) Where any offence under this Act has been committed, the Superintendent of Police within whose jurisdiction such offence has been committed, shall notify all telecommunication service providers, whether public or private, to preserve all records in appropriate data storage form and all such service providers shall be bound to preserve such records in the appropriate data form.

Provided that records under this section shall be preserved for a minimum period of fifty years or after the conclusion of legal proceedings in the concerned case, whichever is later.

Provided further that such preserved records may be destroyed on or after the expiry of the fifty years period, with the prior approval of the Ministry of Home Affairs in the Central Government or in the Government of the State, as the case may be.

66. Right of victim to information during investigation - (1) The Superintendent of Police, or officer designated by him or her shall inform the victim in writing about the progress of investigations into the offence, whether or not the offender has been arrested, charge-sheeted, granted bail, charged, convicted or sentenced, and if a person has been charged with the offence, then the name of the suspected offender.

(2) The victim shall have the right to receive a copy of any statement of the witness recorded during trial, and a copy of all statements and documents filed under Section 173 of the Code of Criminal Procedure, 1973 including the charge-sheet or closure report submitted by police.

67. Information to National Authority or State Authority regarding delayed or biased investigations - (1) A victim or informant aggrieved about any procedure of investigation including the lack of impartiality or fairness, the biased nature or the failure of the investigating agency to receive evidence or examine witnesses in relation to offences committed under the Act shall have the right to make a complaint in this regard to the National Authority or the State Authority constituted under this Act.

(2) Where on a complaint received under sub-Section (1), it appears that there has been a lack of impartiality or fairness or was biased on the part of the investigating agency or that it failed to receive evidence or examine a witness in course of investigation, the National Authority or the State Authority may request the State Government to order a further

investigation or re-investigation in the manner provided under Section 68 to investigate offences under this Act.

68. Further Investigation or re-investigation - (1) Where:

(a) no report under Section 173 of the Code of Criminal Procedure, 1973, is filed within a period of ninety days from the date of recording of information under Section 154 of the Code of Criminal Procedure, 1973; or,

(b) the National Authority or the State Authority on an inquiry made under sub-Section (2) of Section 67 has come to the conclusion that the investigation of an offence under this Act was not carried out in a fair, impartial or unbiased manner requests the State Government to order a further investigation or re-investigation, the investigating officer shall file a report with the Inspector General of Police in relation to the investigation so conducted, giving reasons for the failure to file within the prescribed time, such report as contained in clause (a) or the circumstances leading to the request under clause (b) and action taken thereon.

(2) The report filed under sub-Section (1) shall be reviewed the Directorate of Prosecution where such Directorate is constituted under Section 25A of the Code of Criminal Procedure, 1973, or where no such Directorate is constituted, by a committee constituted by the State Government, headed by an officer of the level of an Inspector General of Police, and which may pass such orders for further investigation or a re-investigation by another officer not below the rank of Deputy Superintendent of Police wherever it comes to the conclusion that, having regard to the nature of investigation already carried out, such investigation would be necessary.

(3) The Directorate of Prosecution or the review committee constituted under sub-Section (2), as the case may be, may also review cases of such offences where the trial ends in acquittal or in an inappropriate sentence and issue orders for filing appeal, wherever required.

69. Judicial inquiry into occurrence of organised communal and targeted violence - (1) Where the offence of organised communal and targeted violence, contained under Section 9, occurs, the State Government shall order an inquiry to be conducted by a Judge of the High Court of the State in which such violence occurs, in addition to the investigation held by the police, into the discharge of public functions by the public servants legally bound to prevent the occurrence of such violence.

(2) The inquiry referred to in sub-Section (1) shall, in no case, commence later than ninety days from the date of occurrence of organised communal and targeted violence.

(3) All the powers under the Commissions of Inquiry Act, 1952 as if the Judge of the High Court were holding an inquiry under the said Act.

(4) The Judge of the High Court holding an inquiry under this Section shall *inter alia* inquire into whether due diligence was exercised by such public servant in the discharge of duty.

(5) Where the Judge of the High Court holding an inquiry under this Section finds upon evidence that the conduct of the public servant constitutes dereliction of duty as defined under this Act, he or she shall direct that information be recorded under section 154, Code of Criminal Procedure, 1973, against such public servant.

EVIDENCE

70. Evidentiary standard for sexual assault - Upon the sole testimony of the victim of sexual assault, the Designated Judge appointed under this Act may conclude that an offence of sexual assault has been committed by the accused against the said victim.

Provided that in a prosecution for the offence of sexual assault, it shall not be permissible to put questions in the cross-examination of the victim as to his or her general immoral character or to rely on any evidence of such victim's previous sexual conduct.

71. Inference from nature and circumstances of the act - Where any question arises whether an offence committed against a member of a group was committed against him or her by virtue of his or her membership of a group, it shall be inferred that it was so directed from the nature and circumstances of the act.

72. Presumptions as to offences under this Act - (1) If in a prosecution for any offence committed under this Act, it is shown that the accused committed or abetted or conspired to commit the offence of hate propaganda under section 8, it shall be presumed, unless the contrary is proved, that the offence committed was knowingly directed against a person by virtue of his or her membership of a group.

(2) Whenever an offence of organised communal and targeted violence is committed and it is shown that a hostile environment against a group exists or the offence of hate propaganda under section 8 was committed against a group, it shall be presumed, unless the contrary isproved, that the said offence was knowingly directed against persons belonging to the group by virtue of their membership of the group.

INITIATION OF PROCEEDINGS

73. Waiver of immunity - (1) Save and excepting those provided under the Constitution or under this Act, immunities or special procedural rules which may attach to the official capacity of any person, shall not bar any proceedings under this Act.

(2) The defence of sovereign immunity will not be available for offences committed under this Act.

74. Sanction not required for certain offences - The provision of Section 196 and 197 of the Code of Criminal Procedure, 1973 shall not apply to offences by public servants under Schedule III and the Designated Judge may take cognizance of such offence when satisfied that the said offence has been committed.

Provided that prosecution of an offence by a public servant other than those requiring sanction under section 196 and 197 of the Code of Criminal Procedure, 1973 shall not be held up for want of sanction for a related offence by the same public servant.

75. Prosecution for offences by the state and public servants - (1) Where an application for sanction for prosecution of a public servant has been made under Section 196 and 197 of the Code of Criminal Procedure, 1973 and the Central Government in relation to the Union Territories or the State Government, as the case may be, does not communicate the order granting or refusing sanction to prosecute such public servant within a period of thirty days from the date on which such application is made, the sanction applied for shall be deemed to have been granted on the expiration of the said period of thirty days and the Designated Judge appointed under this Act shall take cognizance of any offence under this Act.

(2) For the purposes of sub-Section (1), sanction shall not be refused, except with reasons to be recorded in writing.

76. Special Public Prosecutors - (1) For every State, the concerned State Government shall, by notification in the official gazette, appoint a panel of Special Public Prosecutors for prosecuting offences under this Act, and who shall be deemed to be Special Public Prosecutors under sub-Section (8) of Section 24 of the Code of Criminal Procedure, 1973 within the meaning of clause (u) of Section 2 thereof.

(2) Special Public Prosecutors shall conduct the prosecution of offences under this Act in a fair and impartial manner and in the interest of justice. In the event the Special Public Prosecutor conducts the prosecution in a biased manner against the interest of the informant or

the victim, the State Government may, on its own or on information received from a victim or informant, replace the Special Public Prosecutor.

DESIGNATED JUDGES

77. Power to appoint Designated Judges - (1) The Central Government in relation to the Union Territories or the State Government may, by notification in the Official Gazette appoint as many Designated Judges in consultation with the Chief Justice of the High Court as it may be necessary for such case or group of cases as may be specified in the notification to try the following offences:

(a) any offence punishable under this Act; and

(b) any conspiracy to commit or any attempt to commit or any abetment of any of the offences specified in clause (a).

(2) Notwithstanding anything contained in sub-Section (1), if, having regard to the exigencies of the situation prevailing in a State, the Government is of the opinion that it is expedient to appoint, Additional Designated Judges outside the State, for the trial of such offences specified under sub-Section (1), the trial whereof within the State –

(a) is not likely to be fair or impartial or completed with utmost dispatch; or

(b) is not likely to be feasible without occasioning a breach of peace or grave risk to the safety of the accused, the witnesses, the Public Prosecutor and the Judge or any of them; or

(c) is not otherwise in the interests of justice,

it may request the Central Government to appoint, in relation to such offences under sub-Section (1), an Additional Designated Judge outside the State and thereupon the Central Government may, after taking into account the information furnished by the State Government and making such inquiry, if any, as it may deem fit, appoint, by notification, such Additional Designated Judge at such place outside the State as may be specified in the notification.

(3) A person shall not be qualified for appointment as a Designated Judge or Additional Designated Judge under this Act unless he or she is or has been a Sessions Judge under the Code of Criminal Procedure, 1973.

78. Cases triable by Designated Judges - (1) Notwithstanding anything contained in the Code of Criminal Procedure, 1973, or in any other law for the time being in force, the offences specified under this Act shall be tried by Designated Judges appointed under this Act.

(2) Every offence specified under this Act shall be tried by the Designated Judge for the area within which it was committed, or, as the

case may be, by the Designated Judge appointed for the case, or where there are more Designated Judges than one for such area, by such one of them as may be specified in this behalf by the State Government.

(3) When trying the accused person, a Designated Judge may also try any offence, other than an offence specified under this Act, with which the accused may, under the Code of Criminal Procedure, 1973, be charged at the same trial if the offence is connected with the offence under this Act. 31.

(4) If, in the course of any trial under this Act, it is found that the accused person has committed any offence, the Special Court may, whether such offence is or is not an offence under this Act, convict such person of such offence and pass any sentence authorised by law for the punishment thereof.

(5) Notwithstanding anything contained in the Code of Criminal Procedure, 1973, a Designated Judge shall hold the trial of an offence on day-to-day basis save and except for reasons beyond the control of anyone.

79. Procedure and power of the Designated Judge - (1) A Designated Judge, appointed under this Act may take cognizance of offences without the accused being committed to him or her for trial.

(2) In trying the accused persons, the Designated Judge shall follow the procedure for the trial of warrant cases prescribed by the Code of Criminal Procedure, 1973.

(3) Save as provided in sub-Sections (1) or sub-Section (2), the provisions of the Code of Criminal Procedure, 1973, shall, so far as they are not inconsistent with this Act, apply to the proceedings before a Designated Judge; and for the purposes of the said provisions, the Court of the Designated Judge shall be deemed to be a Court of Session and the person conducting a prosecution before a Designated Judge shall be deemed to be a Special Public Prosecutor as provided under this Act.

(4) A Designated Judge may pass upon any person convicted by him or her any sentence authorised under this Act for the punishment of the offence of which such person is convicted.

80. Attachment of property - (1) Where the charge has been framed in relation to an offence under this Act, the Designated Judge may direct that the property of the accused person, which has been gained by him or her as a result of the commission of that offence, to be attached during the pendency of the trial and until conviction or acquittal, as the case may be.

(2) The provision under Section 60 of the Code of Civil Procedure, 1908 shall apply in relation to property being attached under this section.

81. Sale of attached property on conviction - Where upon conviction, the Designated Judge imposes a fine in addition to any other sentence under this Act, he or she may direct the property attached under Section 80 to be sold and proceeds thereof to be paid and the amount so recovered be applied in defraying the expenses properly incurred by the Central Government or the State Government in discharge of its functions under Sections 89, 90, 95, 96, and 104 of this Act.

82. Removal of person likely to commit an offence under this Act - (1) Where a Designated Judge is satisfied, *suo moto* or upon a complaint or a police report that a person is likely to commit an offence under this Act in any area in a State, it may, by order in writing, direct such person to remove himself or herself beyond the limit of such area, by such route and within such time as may be specified in the order, and not to return to that area from which he or she was directed to remove himself or herself for such period, not exceeding six months, as may be specified in the order.

(2) The Designated Judge shall, along with the order under sub-Section (1), communicate to the person directed under that sub-Section the grounds on which such order has been made.

(3) The Designated Judge may revoke or modify the order made under sub-Section (1), for the reasons to be recorded in writing, on the representation made by the person against whom such order has been made or by any other person on his or her behalf within thirty days from the date of the order.

83. Rights of victims during trial under this Act - (1) It shall be the duty and responsibility of the State for making arrangements for the protection of victims, and witnesses against any kind of intimidation, coercion or inducement or violence or threats of violence.

(2) A victim shall be treated with fairness, respect and dignity and with due regard to any special need that arises because of the victim's age or gender or educational disadvantage or poverty.

(3) A victim shall have the right to reasonable, accurate, and timely notice of any court proceeding including any bail proceeding.

Provided that the Special Public Prosecutor or the State Government shall inform the victim about any proceedings under this Act.

(4) A victim shall have the right to apply to the Court to summon parties for production of any documents or material witnesses or examine persons present.

(5) A victim shall be entitled to be heard at any proceeding under this Act in respect of bail, discharge, release, parole, conviction or sentence of an accused or any connected proceedings or arguments and file written submissions on conviction, acquittal or sentencing.

(6) A victim shall be entitled to receive free legal aid and to engage any advocate who he or she chooses from among those enrolled in the legal aid panel under the Legal Services Authorities Act, 1987 or any other advocate of their choice and the Legal Aid Services Authority established under the said Act shall pay all costs, expenses and fees of the advocate appointed by the victim or informant at a rate not less than the fees payable to the Special Public Prosecutor.

84. Protection of victims, informants and witnesses - (1) Notwithstanding anything contained in the Code of Criminal Procedure, 1973, the Designated Judge trying a case under this Act shall provide to a victim, informant or witness complete protection to secure the ends of justice.

(2) Without prejudice to the generality of sub-Section (1), such protection for the victim, informant or witness may extend to the following provisions:

(a) relocation;

(b) travelling and maintenance expenses during investigation and trial; and,

(c) social-economic rehabilitation during investigation and trial.

(3) The State shall inform the concerned Designated Judge under sub-Section (1) of Section 77 about the protection provided to any victim, informant or witnesses and the Designated Judge shall periodically review the protection being offered under this Section and pass appropriate orders.

(4) Without prejudice to the generality of the provisions of sub-Section (1), a Designated Judge may, on an application made by a victim, informant or witness in any proceedings before it or by the Special Public Prosecutor in relation to such victim, informant or witness or on its own motion, take such measures including:

(a) not mentioning the names and addresses of the witnesses in its orders or judgements or in any records of the case accessible to the public;

(b) issuing directions for non-disclosure of the identity and addresses of the witnesses;

(c) immediately dealing with any complaint of harassment of a victim, informant or witness and on the same day, pass appropriate orders for protection;

Provided that inquiry or investigation into the complaint received under clause (c) shall be tried separately from the main case by the Designated Judge and concluded within six months from the date of receipt of the complaint;

Provided further that where the complaint under clause (c) is against any public servant, the court shall forthwith restrain such public servant from interfering with the victim, informant or witness, as the case may be, in any matter related or unrelated to the pending case, except with the specific permission of the Designated Judge.

(5) It shall be the duty of the Investigating Officer and the Station House Officer to record the complaint of victim, informant or witnesses against any kind of intimidation, coercion or inducement or violence or threats of violence, whether given orally or in writing, and a copy of the same shall be sent to the State Authority within twenty-four hours of recording it. A victim shall also be entitled to lodge the said complaint with the District legal Services Authority.

(6) The officers in charge of the District Legal Services Authority upon receipt of any complaint under sub-Section (5) shall forward the same to the concerned Designated Judge within twenty-four hours.

(7) The Member of the State Authority, if such a Member is available preferably from the concerned district, shall visit the office of the District Legal Services Authority once in a week to monitor complaints of intimidation, coercion or violence on victim, informant or witness and scrutinise the follow-up action taken on the same. To ensure effective follow up action and protection, the said Member of the State Authority shall have the power to move the concerned Designated Judge as and when required.

85. Record of court proceedings - All proceedings related to offences under this Act shall be video recorded.

86. Appeal and revision - (1) Subject to the provisions of this Act, the High Court may exercise, so far as they may be applicable, all powers of appeal and revision conferred by the Code of Criminal Procedure, 1973, on a High Court as if the court of the Designated Judge were a Court of Session trying cases within local limits of the High Court.

(2) Every appeal under this section shall be preferred within sixty days from the date of the judgement, sentence or order.

Provided that the High Court having jurisdiction may entertain an appeal after the expiry of the said sixty days, if it is satisfied that the appellant had sufficient cause for not preferring the appeal within the said period of sixty days.

CHAPTER VII

REMEDY AND REPARATIONS

87. Right to remedy and reparations - (1) Any person, whether or not he or she belongs to a group as defined under this Act, who has suffered physical, mental, psychological or monetary harm or harm to his or her property as a result of the commission of any offence under this Act, or when death has occurred as a consequence thereof, the next of kin of such deceased person shall be entitled to remedy and reparations including compensation, restitution and rehabilitation as applicable to them in accordance with the provisions under this Chapter.

(2) Where the death of any person has occurred as a consequence of the commission of an offence under this Act, the compensation for such death shall be paid to the next of kin being the wife or husband, as the case may be, parent and child, if any, and shall be divided amongst the before-mentioned parties, or any of them, in equal parts.

88. Duty to provide remedy and reparations - (1) The State Government through the office of the Collector shall provide remedy and reparations including compensation, restitution and rehabilitation to all persons entitled under Section 87 in accordance with the provisions of this Chapter.

(2) Notwithstanding anything contained in this Act, or under any other law for the time being in force, it shall be the duty of each Collector, either by himself or herself or through his or her subordinates, to ensure that there is adequate supervision and control over the performance of the obligations under this Chapter.

89. Duty to ensure immediate safety of persons and property - (1) The State Government in co-ordination with the Chief-Secretary of the State, the Inspector General of Police, Superintendents of Police or Commissioner of Police, as the case may be, and the Collector shall ensure that any person mentioned under Section 87, whose life, liberty or property is threatened, or where he or she apprehends such threat, is immediately provided security including creating police outposts and pickets in the vicinity of the affected area and providing temporary relocation if necessary.

(2) The State Government and the Collector shall ensure that that all properties of such person mentioned in Section 87, whether moveble or immovable are protected, in particular, against destruction, vandalism, appropriation, occupation, waste, damage, alienation, misuse, sale or transfer by any means.

(3) Any alienation of property of such persons attributable to communal and targeted violence referred to in sub-Section (2) shall be void.

90. Establishment of Relief Camps - (1) When organised communal and targeted violence occurs, the State Government shall establish relief camps in safe locations for the internally displaced persons.

Provided that such relief camps shall not be closed unless all internally displaced persons have been voluntarily rehabilitated in accordance with section 96.

(2) A relief camps established under sub-Section (1) shall continue to be operated by the State Government until all internally displaced persons residing in that relief camp return to their original habitations, or are resettled in a new suitable location.

(3) Relief camps established under sub-Section (1) shall, at the minimum, regardless of the circumstances and without discrimination, provide the internally displaced persons with:

(a) basic shelter which is appropriate and adequate to protect the residents of the camps from extremes of the weather, and which provides due privacy especially to women and girls;

(b) 24 hours security at the relief camp;

(c) adequate nutritious and culturally appropriate food;

(d) potable drinking water;

(e) adequate clothing which is culturally appropriate and sufficient to protect the residents of the camp from extremes of weather;

(f) essential medical services including antenatal and postnatal care of expectant mothers, paediatric care and emergency and rehabilitative services for the injured and referral services wherever necessary;

(g) adequate sanitation;

(h) psycho-social and trauma counselling and psychiatric services;

(i) child-care services for infants and small children;

(j) educational facilities for children;

(k) special facilities and assistance, as may be necessary and reasonable for the medical condition and treatment of certain residents of the relief camps, such as children, especially unaccompanied minors, expectant mothers, mothers with young children, female heads of households, elderly and disabled persons with special needs;

(l) full access to members of the National Authority and State Authority.

91. Duties in relation to relief camps - Until such time internally displaced persons are located in relief camps, it shall be duty of the State Government and, in particular, the Collector, either by himself or herself or through his or her subordinates to ensure the following:

(a) an environment free from any exposure to or occurrence of any form of sexual assault, exploitation, intimidation, violence, or forced labour in the relief camps;

(b) provision for family members of one household unit to remain in the same relief camp or if they wish, relocate together to another relief camp, or if separated, then to enable them to reunite as soon as possible by taking all steps to expedite the location and reunion of such families, particularly children and parents;

(c) establishment of a single window system to complete all administrative formalities in relation to provision of quick relief and rehabilitation, including making available identity documents, certificates, ration cards, passports, speedy disposal of insurance and other claims, provision for certification of loss or damage of educational or other certificates or ownership or other documents in respect of all such persons;

(d) restoration of all official documents of all such persons that include but are not limited to ration cards, property proofs, government cards and identities, school and college related documents, election cards at the earliest but in any case not later than three months shall be the responsibility of the State Government;

(e) facilitation for the students affected by organised communal and targeted violence to appear for any examination, condoning delays caused by such violence, and to provide for such facilitation, including creating support centres for the same.

(f) provision for victims to file information in relation to offences under this Act and record statements in pursuance of any complaints related to organised communal and targeted violence;

(g) provision for all internally displaced persons to claim and receive compensation while still in the relief camps;

(h) provision of a single window system for all internally displaced persons to make enquiries and give information about the status and whereabouts of missing family members, relatives or friends and assist them in receiving such information as desired with regard to the progress of investigation of the whereabouts and condition of such missing persons;

(i) access to legal aid in the prosecution of offences under this Act.

Provided that special efforts shall be made to ensure the full participation of the internally displaced persons residing in the relief camps and, in particular, women, in the planning and distribution of basic services and supplies;

Provided further that such assistance may be organised with the help of individuals and groups including human rights groups, and professionals or groups qualified in the providing specialised services to such persons including women's groups, child rights groups and support groups of persons mentioned under Section 87.

92. State Assessment Committee - (1) A State Assessment Committee shall be formed in each State by the appropriate Government to assess aspects of reparations in the event of occurrence of organised communal and targeted violence.

(2) The State Assessment Committee under sub-Section (1) shall comprise the following:

(a) Chairperson of State Human Rights Commission - **Chairperson,** *ex-officio*

(b) Chief Secretary of the State - **Member**

(c) Member of a human rights organisation approved by the National Authority - **Member**

93. Functions of the State Assessment Committee - The State Assessment Committee shall perform the following functions:

(a) duly inform all internally displaced persons, including those affected by the organised communal and targeted violence, whether or not residing in a relief camp, of the procedure and the purpose of the assessment;

(b) conduct, in accordance with Section 94, a survey of the injury to life and property in relation to offences committed under this Act for the purposes of restitution in the affected area;

(c) prepare, in accordance with Section 95, a list of internally displaced persons including any person mentioned under Section 87, identified through the survey so conducted;

(d) assess and certify loss or damage caused by organised communal and targeted violence for the purposes of Section 96;

(e) appropriately rehabilitate restoring all rights of and provision of services to all persons entitled under Section 87 in accordance with section 96;

(f) make an assessment, including gathering of necessary data and information, at the site of violence of damage to life, liberty and property;

(g) prepare a budget including estimated expenditure of various components of rehabilitation and resettlement activities or programmes in consultation with representatives of the affected families.

94. Survey by State Assessment Committee - (1) Every survey by the State Assessment Committee under clause (b) of Section 93 shall contain the following area-wise (village or locality), as the State Assessment Committee may deem fit, information of all internally displaced persons including any person entitled under Section 87, whether or not he or she resides in a relief camp, namely:—

(a) families including dependants belonging to a group who are permanently residing, engaged in any trade, business, occupation or vocation in the area affected by organised communal and targeted violence;

(b) families including dependants that have lost or have been displaced from their place of ordinary residence, agricultural land, estate, employment or are alienated wholly or substantially from the main source of their trade, business, occupation or vocation;

(c) agricultural labourers, non-agricultural labourers, professionals, businessmen etc;

(d) the disabled, destitute, orphans, widows, elderly or any other category of persons deemed particularly vulnerable in the circumstances because they are not provided or cannot immediately be provided with alternative livelihood, and who are not otherwise covered as part of a family;

(e) means of alternative livelihood where there is a situation of social, political or economic boycott;

(f) possibilities of conflict and effect thereof especially on youth and children in the event of their translocation;

(2) While conducting the survey and undertaking assessment under sub-Section (1), the State Assessment Committee shall take into consideration the impact of organised communal and targeted violence on the assets and infrastructure, applicable municipal tax, applicable circle rate tax of the locality, drainage, sanitation, sources of drinking water, sources of water, for cattle, community ponds, grazing land, plantations, public utilities, such as post offices, fair price shops, food storage godowns, electricity supply, health care facilities, schools and educational or training facilities, places of worship, burial and cremation grounds, livelihood options.

(3) The survey and assessment shall be completed within a period of forty-five days from the date of the constitution of the State Assessment Committee and all infrastructural and other facilities as required by the State Assessment Committee shall be provided by the State Government without any delay.

95. Registration of persons injured by organised communal and targeted violence - (1) The State Assessment Committee shall register the names of all persons who have suffered injury as a result of offences under Section 9, including internally displaced persons and those mentioned under Section 87, when information relating to the commission of such an offence is recorded.

(2) The registration of persons mentioned under sub-Section (1) shall be made within fifteen days of the appointment of the State Assessment Committee and issued an appropriate identity-card to avail measures under this Chapter.

(3) Where any person is aggrieved by the non-inclusion of his or her name in the list of persons entitled prepared by the State Assessment Committee under sub-Section (1), he or she may approach the State Assessment Committee with the request to include his or her name in such a list and the State Assessment Committee, if satisfied that the

aggrieved person is a victim or internally displaced person or entitled under Section 87, shall add the said name to the list so prepared.

(4) Where any person is aggrieved by the refusal of the State Assessment Committee to include his or her name in the list so prepared under sub-Section (1), he or she may prefer an appeal to the National Authority under clause (b) of Section 29.

96. Restitution and rehabilitation - (1) The State Government shall ensure reparations to internally displaced persons, whether or not such persons are residing in a relief camp or to any person entitled under Section 87 by adopting measures for restitution and implementing comprehensive rehabilitation plans.

Provided that the process of rehabilitation shall ensure full participation of such persons.

Provided further that the rehabilitation of such persons be declared by them to be entirely voluntary.

Provided further that the rehabilitation as provided in this section, to be made in consultation with the National Authority.

Provided further that the State Government shall make the said reparations on the basis of the survey conducted by the State Assessment Committee under Section 94.

(2) Restitution and rehabilitation shall include:

(a) resettlement of the family or persons entitled under Section 95 in homes, dwellings and places of livelihood affected by organised communal and targeted violence, either in the existing locations or such new locations, as the case may be, by restoring them to levels not less than those prevailing before such violence occurred or fresh construction of the same in new resettlement colonies or allocation of suitable land for the same;

(b) restoration of employment or provision of alternate employment, including the tools or means of livelihood and provision of soft loans where necessary;

(c) restoration and repair of places of worship or sacred sites damaged or destroyed during the commission of the said offence under this Act and construction of places of worship in resettlement colonies as requested by such persons enlisted under Section 95;

(d) restoration of all civic amenities in and around the original habitations at least equivalent to those prevailing before the occurrence of organised communal and targeted violence, or provision of civic amenities in new resettlement sites or colonies, as the case may be;

(e) reconstruction to their original condition, all community structures, including schools and health centers and means of livelihood destroyed or damaged, during commission of offences under this Act, or construction of new community structures in resettlement sites and colonies, as the case may be;

(f) long-term psychological counselling for all and particularly, to victims of sexual assault;

(g) necessary and appropriate provisions for rehabilitation of women, including community-based rehabilitation of those widowed;

(h) appropriate provisions for rehabilitation of children identified in the list under Section 95 including community-based rehabilitation for those orphaned and appropriate arrangements for their continuing education.

97. Duty to establish conditions to enable return - The Central Government in relation to the Union Territories or the State Government, as the case may be, shall establish conditions and provide means to enable internally displaced persons enlisted under Section 95 to return to their place of ordinary residence or livelihood in safety and with dignity, protected against any threat, intimidation or attack to their life, liberty or property, provided that;

(a) such return shall in all cases be declared by such persons to be entirely voluntary;

(b) the concerned public authorities shall ensure the full participation of all persons residing in the relief camp in the planning and management of their return or resettlement.

98. Powers to summon witnesses and take evidence - In addition to the powers conferred by the Act, the State Assessment Committee shall have the same powers as are vested in a Civil Court under the Code of Civil Procedure, 1908, while carrying out their functions, in respect of the following matters, namely-

(a) summoning and enforcing the attendance of witnesses and examining them on oath;

(b) discovery and production of any document;

(c) receiving evidence on affidavits;

(d) issuing commissions for the examination of witnesses or documents;

(e) any other matter which may be prescribed.

99. Compensation - (1) It shall be the duty of the Central Government in relation to the Union Territories or the State Government, as the case may be, to provide appropriate compensation in accordance with Schedule IV and as assessed under this Act by the District Assessment Committee established under sub-Section (1) of Section 104, to any person mentioned under Section 87 or any internally displaced person, whether or not such person resides in a relief camp, in accordance with principles under Section 100.

(2) Compensation under sub-Section (1) shall be made in the following manner:

(a) Within thirty days of the date of the incident of communal or targeted violence, whether organised or not, a minimum ex-gratia compensation in accordance with the Schedule IV of this Act.

Provided that no compensation for injury resulting in death shall be less than rupees fifteen lakhs;

Provided further that the concerned government in the case of a minor shall, and in the case of a woman may, with the consent of such woman, dispense the awarded ex-gratia compensation by way of a monthly pension deposited in a bank account in the name of the minor or such woman, as the case may be.

Provided further that in case of need, the guardian of the minor may apply to the District Court to withdraw the money.

Provided further that compensation under Schedule IV shall be revised every three years by the Central Government in consultation with the National Authority and the said revision shall be published by notification in the Official Gazette;

(b) In addition to the compensation paid under clause (a) above, compensation shall be payable to such person as determined by the District Assessment Committee in accordance with the provisions contained in this Chapter.

Provided that for the determination of such additional compensation, the Central Government shall by rules create a multiplier method of arriving at compensation or any other method known to law taking into consideration Section 101.

100. Principles for assessment of compensation - (1) While determining compensation under clause (b) of sub-Section (2) of Section 99, the District Assessment Committee, shall not discriminate against persons entitled under Section 87, including those registered under Section 95, on grounds of religion, race, caste, sex, place of birth or any of them.

(2) The amount of compensation under this Act shall be such that a person is restored to levels of housing, habitat, means of livelihood and economic standards including all social and civic facilities, which are at par or better than those that he or she enjoyed before the commission of an offence under this Act.

(3) While determining compensation under clause (b) of sub-Section (2) of Section 99, the District Assessment Committee, shall take into consideration the gravity of the violation of rights and the compensation shall be proportional to the gravity thereof.

(4) Subject to sub-Section (3), a reasonable compensation for loss due to injury to the property, shall be awarded to such person so as to enable him or her to reconstruct or restore his or her property to its original condition.

101. Compensation to be made for - The assessment of compensation, in addition to compensation paid under Schedule IV, shall be made for:

(a) injury to public property;

(b) injury to private property;

(c) bodily injury caused to a person or death;

(d) moral injury;

(e) material injury and loss of earnings, including lost opportunities of employment, education and social benefits;

(f) psychological injury caused to such person;

(g) cost of the actions by the authorities and police to take preventive and other actions;

(h) required for legal or expert assistance, medicine and medical services, and psychological and social services.

102. District Assessment Committee - (1) The State Government shall, by notification, establish a District Assessment Committee in respect of each district in the State, to perform such functions assigned to it under this Act and to assist the State Assessment Committee in the performance of its functions.

(2) The District Assessment Committee shall consist of the following members, namely –

(a) Collector or District Magistrate or Deputy Commissioner, as the case may be, of the district - **Chairperson,** *ex-officio.*

(b) Chief Medical Officer of the district - **Member**

(c) Judicial Magistrate - **Member**

(d) One respectable citizen belonging to a group - **Member**

Provided that, at all times, at least one Member, including the Chairperson, shall be a woman.

103. Functions of the District Assessment Committee - (1) The District Assessment Committee shall perform functions assigned to it under this Act and shall coordinate with various departments and existing bodies like the National Disaster Management Authority to take all measures to provide reparations under this Act.

(2) Subject to any general or special order of the appropriate Government, the District Assessment Committee shall perform the following functions, namely:-

(a) supervise establishment of relief camps in accordance with provisions of this Chapter;

(b) ensure and enable safe passage of internally displaced persons from the site of violence to a temporary shelter or relief camp, established by the State Government;

(c) ensure participation of internally displaced persons in the formulation of rehabilitation and resettlement plans;

(d) verify facts and ensure full and public disclosure of the truth to the extent that such disclosure does not cause further harm or threaten the safety and interests of such person, witnesses, or persons who have intervened to assist the victim or prevent the occurrence of further violations;

(e) perform such other functions as the State Government or the State Assessment Committee may, from time to time, by order in writing, assign.

104. Authority to determine and disburse compensation - (1) For the purposes of determining compensation under this section, the District Assessment Committee shall include a District Judge who shall be the Chairperson of the District Assessment Committee.

(2) In addition to the compensation paid under Schedule IV, the District Assessment Committee constituted under sub-Section (1) shall determine the quantum of compensation to be paid to a person entitled under Section 87, in accordance with principles provided under Section 100.

(3) The entitlement based on the assessment done by the District Assessment Committee constituted under sub-Section (1) under sub-Section (2) shall be provided as a certificate along with a statement of the list of entitlement to such victim or affected person and the timeframe for disbursement shall be notified.

(4) The amount payable under sub-Sections (2) shall be disbursed by the State Government, not later than fifteen days from the date of grant of certificate by the District Assessment Committee unless an extended period is notified for reasons beyond the control of the State Government.

105. Appeal from assessment - (1) Any person entitled to relief under Section 87 not satisfied with the assessment made by the District Assessment Committee under Section 104, may appeal to the High Court of the State concerned in the manner provided by rules under the Act.

106. Rights of persons under this Chapter - (1) Any person entitled to relief under Section 87 shall be informed orally and in writing by the District Assessment Committee about procedures for obtaining compensation for harm suffered as a result of organised communal and targeted violence or any other offence under this Act respectively, and extend all assistance to such person to make his or her claim in accordance with the provisions of this Act.

(2) There shall be counselling and protection of women and children against misuse and intimidation resulting from receipts of cash compensation.

(3) In case of any default in the timely disbursal of compensation under Section 104, persons mentioned under sub-Section (1) shall have the right to complain to the National Authority or the State Authority, which shall monitor these complaints till final resolution of claims.

107. Subrogation of Rights - (1) Upon payment of compensation, the Central Government in relation to the Union Territories or the State Government, as the case may be, will stand subrogated to the rights of all persons entitled under Section 87 and shall be entitled to claim the said amount from the persons responsible for the loss of life, liberty or property or any other loss in accordance with law.

108. Claim on behalf of the Central Government and State Government - For the purpose of making an assessment of loss or damage caused by the organised communal and targeted violence under sub-Section (2) of Section 94, the State Assessment Committee shall consider the following:

(a) expenses of the Government, authorities under the control of the Government, local authorities and institutions for expenses incurred in providing relief and rehabilitation to the persons enlisted under Section 95;

(b) administration expenses incurred by the Central Government or the State Government or local authorities to cope with the organised communal and targeted violence, including all local and administrative expenses attributable or related to such organised communal and targeted violence;

(c) expenses related to loss of revenue to Government and authorities under the control of the Government or local authorities arising out of, or connected with to such organised communal and targeted violence;

(d) expenses on account of damage to the fauna including milch and drought animals;

(e) expenses arising from damage to flora including destruction of agricultural crops, vegetables, trees and orchards;

(f) expenses on account of damage to environment including pollution of soil, flora, fauna and water systems;

(g) expenses relating to loss and destruction of property;

(h) expenses relating to loss of business or employment or both;

(i) expenses in respect of injuries that are likely to be suffered on account of the organised communal and targeted violence;

(j) any other expenses or expenses which the State Assessment Committee may determine for reasons to be recorded in writing as arising out of, or connected with the organised communal and targeted violence.

109. Establishment of Communal and Targeted Violence Relief and Rehabilitation Fund - (1) The Central Government shall make available, on the advice of the National Authority, funds from the Consolidated Fund of India, a Communal and Targeted Violence Relief and Rehabilitation Fund for immediate disbursement of compensation for immediate rehabilitation and reparation, and such funds made available shall be recoverable from monies as may be payable to the State Governments by the Central Government.

(2) The amount in the said fund shall be applied by the State Assessment Committee and the District Assessment Committee, as the case may be, for the following purposes:

(a) disbursal of amounts in settlement of claims registered with the District Assessment Committee.

(b) apportionment of part of the fund for the relief, rehabilitation and reparations provided for under the Act.

(3) "Funds" will be fines that may be levied under this Act.

110. Guarantee of non-repetition - It shall be the duty of the Central Government and the State Governments to make and take all steps to ensure satisfaction and guarantees of non-repetition of offences under this Act and which shall include, where applicable, any or all of the following:

(a) Cessation of continuing violations;

(b) The search for the bodies of those killed or disappeared and assistance in the identification and reburial of the bodies in accordance with the cultural practices of the families and communities;

(c) Ensure access to justice to the victims;

(d) Commemorations and tributes to the victims;

(e) Preventing the recurrence of violations by such means as:

(i) protecting persons in the legal, media and other related professions and human rights defenders;

(ii) conducting and strengthening, on a priority and continued basis, human rights training to all sectors of society, in particular to military and security forces and to law enforcement officials;

(iii) promoting the observance of codes of conduct and ethical norms, in particular international standards, by public servants, including law enforcement, correctional, media, medical, psychological, social service and military personnel, as well as the staff of economic enterprises.

CHAPTER VIII

PENALTIES

111. Punishment for sexual assault - Whoever commits an act of sexual assault, shall be punishable-

(a) where the act is contained in sub-clause (i) of clause (a) of Section 6 and clause (i) of clause (b) of section 7, with rigorous imprisonment for a term which shall not be less than seven years but which may be for life and shall also be liable to fine.

(b) where the act is contained in section sub-clause (ii) of clause (a) of section 7, with rigorous imprisonment for a term which shall not be less than ten years but which may be for life and shall also be liable to fine.

(c) where the act is contained in sub-clause (iii) of clause (a) of Section 7, rigorous imprisonment for a term a term which shall not be less than fourteen years but which may be for life and shall also be liable to fine.

(d) where the act is contained in sub-clauses (ii) to (vi) of clause (b) of Section 7, rigorous imprisonment for a term which shall not be less than seven years but which may extent to ten years and shall also be liable to fine.

112. Punishment for hate propaganda - The offence of hate propaganda shall be punishable with imprisonment which may extend to three years or fine or both.

113. Punishment for organised communal and targeted violence - Whoever commits organised communal and targeted violence shall be punished with rigorous imprisonment for life, and shall also be liable to fine.

114. Punishment for aiding financially, materially or in kind the commission of offence under this Act - Whoever is guilty of the offence under Section 10 shall be punished with imprisonment for a term, which may extend to three years, and shall also be liable to fine.

115. Punishment for offences under Schedule II - When offences under Schedule II are committed, they shall be punishable with penalty provided in the Indian Penal Code, 1860.

116. Punishment for torture – Whoever commits torture shall be punishable with rigorous imprisonment for a term which shall not be less than seven years but which may be for life and shall also be liable to fine.

117. Punishment for dereliction of duty - Whoever being a public servant is guilty of dereliction of duty shall be punished with imprisonment for two years which may extend to five years and shall be liable to fine.

118. Punishment for offences by public servants for breach of command responsibility - Whoever is guilty of an offence under Section 14 shall be punishable with rigorous imprisonment for life, when such failure relates to organised targeted violence and in any other case with imprisonment for a term of ten years and fine.

119. Punishment for offences by other superiors for breach of command responsibility - Whoever is guilty of an offence under Section 15 shall be punishable with rigorous imprisonment for life, when such failure relates to organised targeted violence and in any other case with imprisonment for a term of ten years and fine.

120. Punishment for attempt - Whoever attempts to commit any offence punishable under this Act or causes such attempt to be committed and in such attempt does any act towards the commission of the offence shall be punishable with the punishment provided for the offence.

121. Punishment for abetment - Whoever abets any offence under this Act, if the act abetted is committed in consequence of the abetment, shall be punished with punishment provided for that offence.

122. Punishment for preparation - If any person makes preparation to do or omits to do anything which constitutes an offence punishable under this Act and from the circumstances of the case it may be reasonably inferred that he or she was determined to carry out his or her intention to commit the offence but had been prevented by circumstances independent of his or her will, he or she shall be punishable with rigorous imprisonment for a term which shall not be less than one-half of the minimum term (if any), but which may extend to one-half of the maximum term of imprisonment with which he or she would have been punishable in the event of his or her having committed such offence, and also with fine which shall not be less than one-half of the minimum amount (if any), of fine with which he or she would have been punishable, but which may extend to one-half of the maximum amount of fine with which he or she would have ordinarily (that is to say in the absence of special reasons) been punishable, in the event aforesaid:

Provided that the court may, for reasons to be recorded in the judgment, impose a higher fine.

123. Acts done by several persons in furtherance of common intention - When a criminal act is done by several persons in furtherance of the common intention of all, each of such persons is liable for that act in the same manner as if it were done by him or her alone.

124. Determination of fines - While determining the quantum of fine, the Designated Judge appointed under this Act shall take into consideration gravity of offence, damage assessed by the State Assessment Committee under Section 94 and compensation paid by the

Central Government or the State Government, as the case may be, under Section 99 and assessed by the District Assessment Committee under Section 104.

125. Other remedies not prejudiced - Penalties provided under this Chapter shall be without prejudice to other remedies that a victim or an affected person may have under any other law for the time being in force.

CHAPTER IX

MISCELLANEOUS

126. Non-applicability of limitation for organised communal and targeted violence - The prosecution for the offence of organised communal and targeted violence under Section 9, and the execution of sentences imposed on account of the said offence shall not be subject to any limitation.

127. Protection of action taken in good faith - No suit or other legal proceeding shall lie against the Central Government, State Government, National Authority or State Authority or any Member thereof or any person acting under the direction either of the Central Government, State Government, National Authority or State Authority in respect of anything which is in good faith done or intended to be done in pursuance of this Act or of any rules or any order made there under or in respect of the publication by or under the authority of the Central Government, State Government, National Authority or State Authority of any report paper or proceedings.

Provided that this Section shall not apply to a public servant accused of dereliction of duty under Section 13.

128. Members and officers to be public servants - Every Member of the National Authority or State Authority and every officer appointed or authorised by the National Authority or State Authority to exercise functions under this Act shall be deemed to be a public servant within the meaning of Section 21 of the Indian Penal Code.

129. Duties of Government - The Central Government, in consultation with the National Authority and the State Government, in consultation with the State Authority, shall take all measures to ensure that:

(a) the provisions of this Act are given wide publicity through public media including the television, radio and the print media at regular intervals;

(b) all public servants including police officers and members of judicial services are given periodic sensitisation and awareness training on the issues addressed by this Act;

(c) effective coordination between the services provided by concerned Ministries and Departments dealing with Law, Home Affairs including law and order, health and human resources to address the issue of communal and targeted violence is established and periodical review of the same is conducted.

130. Power of Central Government to make rules - (1) The Central Government may, by notification, make rules to carry out the provisions of this Act.

(2) In particular and without prejudice to the generality of the foregoing power, such rules may provide for all or any of the following matters namely:-

(a) the salaries and allowances and other terms and conditions of service of the Chairperson, Vice-Chairperson and Members of the National Authority;

(b) the conditions subject to which other administrative, technical and scientific staff may be appointed by the National Authority and the salaries and allowances of officers;

(c) any other function or power of the National Authority;

(d) the form in which the annual statement of accounts is to be prepared by the National Authority; and

(e) any other matter which may be prescribed.

(3) Every rule made under this Act shall be laid, as soon as may be after it is made, before each House of Parliament, while it is in session, for a total period of thirty days which may be comprised in one session or in two or more successive sessions, and if, before the expiry of the session immediately following the session or the successive sessions aforesaid, both Houses agree in making any modification in the rule or both Houses agree that the rule should not be made, the rule shall thereafter have effect only in such modified form or be of no effect, as the case may be; so however, that any such modification or annulment shall be without prejudice to the validity of anything previously done under that rule.

131. Power of State Government to make rules - (1) The State Government may, by notification, make rules to carry out the provisions of this Act.

(2) In particular and without prejudice to the generality of the foregoing power, such rules may provide for all or any of the following matters, namely:

(a) the salaries and allowances and other terms and conditions of service of the members of the State Authority;

(b) the conditions subject to which other administrative, technical and scientific staff may be appointed by the State Authority and the salaries and allowances of officers and other staff of the State Authority;

(c) the form in which the annual statement of accounts is to be prepared by the State Authority.

(3) Every rule made by the State Government under this Section shall be laid, as soon as may be after it is made, before each House of the State Legislature where it consists of two Houses, or where such Legislature consists of one House, before that House.

132. Power of National Authority to make regulations - The National Authority shall have the power to makes reguiations to lay down its own procedure.

133. Power of State Authority to make regulations - The State Authority shall have the power to makes regulations to lay down its own procedure.

134. Power to remove difficulties - (1) If any difficulty arises in giving effect to the provisions of this Act, the Central Government, may by order published in the Official Gazette, make such provisions, not inconsistent with the provisions of this Act as appear to it to be necessary or expedient for removing the difficulty.

Provided that no such order shall be made after the expiry of the period of two years from the date of commencement of this Act.

(2) Every order made under this section shall, as soon as may be after it is made, be laid before each house of Parliament.

135. Act to be in addition to any other law - The provisions of this Act shall be in addition to, and not in derogation of, any other law for the time being in force, and nothing contained herein shall exempt any public servant from any proceeding which might, apart from this Act, be instituted against him or her.

SCHEDULE I

Armed Forces and Security Forces constituted under:

(a) The Air Force Act, 1950 (45 of 1950);

(b) The Army Act, 1950 (46 of 1950);

(c) The Assam Rifles Act, 2006 (47 of 2006);

(d) The Bombay Home Guard Act, 1947;

(e) The Border Security Force Act, 1968 (47 of 1968);

(f) The Central Industrial Security Force Act, 1968 (50 of 1968);

(g) The Central Reserve Police Force Act, 1949 (66 of 1949);

(h) The Coast Guard Act, 1978 (30 of 1978);

(i) The Delhi Special Police Establishment Act, 1946 (25 of 1946);

(j) The Indo-Tibetan Border Police Force Act, 1992 (35 of 1992);

(k) The Navy Act, 1957 (62 of 1957);

(l) The National Investigation Agency Act, 2008 (34 of 2008);

(m) The National Security Guard Act, 1986 (47 of 1986);

(n) The Railway Protection Force Act, 1957 (23 of 1957);

(o) The Sashastra Seema Bal Act, 2007 (53 of 2007);

(p) The Special Protection Group Act, 1988 (34 of 1988);

(q) The Territorial Army Act, 1948 (56 of 1948);

(r) The State police forces (including armed constabulary) constituted under the State laws to aid the civil powers of the State and empowered to employ force during internal disturbances or otherwise including armed forces as defined in clause (a) of Section 2 of the Armed Forces (Special Powers) Act, 1958 (28 of 1958).

SCHEDULE II

Part-A

The Indian Penal Code, 1860 Section	*Description of Offence*
153B	Imputations, assertions prejudicial to national integration
295	Injuring or defiling place of worship with the intent to insult the religion of any class
295A	Deliberate and malicious acts intending to outrage religious feelings of any class by insulting its religion or religious beliefs
296	Disturbing religious assembly
297	Trespassing on burial places, etc.
298	Uttering words, etc. with deliberate intent to wound religious feelings of any person

Index